party people

party people

A COOKBOOK FOR CREATIVE CELEBRATIONS

BRIE LARSON
COURTNEY MCBROOM

Publisher Mike Sanders
Art & Design Director William Thomas
Editorial Director Ann Barton
Executive Editor Olivia Peluso
Assistant Director of Art & Design Becky Batchelor
Associate Editor Brandon Buechley
Editorial Assistant Resham Anand
Food Photographer Ciarra Siller
Lifestyle Photographer Noah Fecks
Food Stylist & Recipe Tester Bee Berrie
Prop Stylists Hannah Lewis & Ethan Lunkenheimer
Illustrator Faye Orlove
Copyeditor Christy Wagner
Proofreaders West Matuszak & Mira S. Park
Indexer Beverlee Day

First American Edition, 2025
Published in the United States by DK Publishing
1745 Broadway, 20th Floor, New York, NY 10019

The authorized representative in the EEA is Dorling Kindersley
Verlag GmbH. Arnulfstr. 124, 80636 Munich, Germany

A catalog record for this book
is available from the Library of Congress.
ISBN 978-0-5939-7002-7

DK books are available at special discounts when purchased
in bulk for sales promotions, premiums, fund-raising, or
educational use. For details, contact SpecialSales@dk.com

Printed and bound in Italy

www.dk.com

This book was made with Forest
Stewardship Council™ certified
paper – one small step in DK's
commitment to a sustainable future.
Learn more at
www.dk.com/uk/information/sustainability

This book is for anyone who ever felt like they weren't invited.

contents

welcome to the party

Brie Larson and Courtney McBroom are Party People, and they've been this way their whole lives. Brie was born in Sacramento, California, to an amazing mother who loved to celebrate. Her get-togethers were (and still are) legendary: From an *Indiana Jones*–themed campout, complete with a two-day archaeological dig and a tomb of candy for Brie's eighth birthday, to an adult soiree that featured a fake art auction of works purchased entirely from Goodwill and cocktails inspired by famous paintings, there was never a cap on fun at her house. At the age of five, Brie told her mom she was born to be an actor. Her mom agreed, and after some careful planning, they loaded up the car, popped a Chicks CD into the stereo, and moved to Los Angeles with "Wide Open Spaces" blasting in the background. A ton of hard work later, all that planning paid off. But no matter where she went—on stage, on a movie set, or anywhere in between—Brie's roots never left her. Her mother had given her the party gene.

Meanwhile, Courtney was coming up in the small Texas town of Wichita Falls. She loved to make things like "black pepper hot dogs" (sliced hot dogs doused in an ungodly amount of black pepper) and "Lawry's mashed potatoes" (mashed potatoes doused in an ungodly amount of Lawry's Seasoned Salt). She would then serve these delicacies to her parents and watch as they pretended to enjoy them. To be clear, none of these dishes were good. She was going for color over taste. The hot dogs had to be *black* and the potatoes *orange.* She was eight years old. Around that time, her grandmother gave her her first cookbook, *The Care Bears' Party Cookbook,* and Courtney hasn't looked back since. Approximately one gazillion Funshine Fizzes and a couple cross-country moves later, she's still living that Care Bears' life in Los Angeles. That's where she and Brie finally crossed paths, and their mutual love of food and parties merged them together.

Like with most friendships worth their salt, we found each other through food—a huge vat of molten queso at a mutual friend's 2016 presidential debate party, to be specific. Brie stood over the stovetop, dipping tortilla chips directly into the pot of cheese that Courtney was melting. It wasn't finished, but no matter: It was love at first bite, and we have been best friends ever since, cruising down life's highway with tasty snacks riding shotgun. We've had great times at restaurants, but our specialty has always been dinner parties. Our weekly *Game of Thrones* viewings were as legendary as the show itself. We hosted a Dornish feast, for example, that included a gunpowder-spiced crown roast (because *who will wear the crown?!*), Coconut Lime Rice Pilaf (page 177), and the flakiest flatbread with turmeric butter that you've ever sunk your teeth into. On a different week, we threw a southern spread fit for the King in the North, which was really just an excuse to fry some chicken and serve it alongside creamy mashed potatoes (thankfully not orange this time), Southern Mac 'n' Cheese (the kind with garlic toast crunchies on top; page 137), and maple pecan pull-apart bread.

By the time *Game of Thrones* ended, we had only just begun. One year, Courtney absolutely needed to throw herself a *Dirty Dancing*–themed birthday party, so we made a family-style bowl of "Spaghetti Arms" (a simple pasta limone), a watermelon salad dubbed "I Carried a Watermelon," and pork ribs doused in Swayze Sauce (a sexier version of regular barbecue sauce; page 42). We ate it all and then boogied the night away with our pals. We've spent countless weekends in Ojai and Palm Springs with no agenda other than to grill stuff, drink margaritas, and play board games. And don't forget our annual Hot Dog Appreciation Club Festival, which celebrates the greatest food

LOOK HOW CUTE WE WERE!

group of all, hot dogs. (Read more about this on page 218.) And although our debate over whether a hot dog is a sandwich will never end—Courtney *knows* it is, yet Brie emphatically disagrees—we can agree on most everything else when it comes to food, especially this: It always tastes best when you're surrounded by friends. That's the reason we wrote this book. We want to inspire you to party with your people, and to be honest, it's really not that big of an ask.

People have partied since the beginning of time. *Homo sapiens* and Neanderthals loved to get down, and we've got the cave paintings to prove it. The Mesopotamians weren't ones to refuse a party, either. As the world's first recorded civilization, they invented the New Year's soiree and called it Akitu. The ancient Egyptians invented the dinner table around 2500 BCE and then went on to establish their annual Feast of Drunkenness, also known as Tekh. They're still talking about the debauchery of those nights. The ancient Greeks and Etruscans had symposia, and the ancient Romans bacchanal-ed their brains out. Today, we have sobremesas, powwows, luaus, boodles, crawfish boils, and clam bakes. Indeed, from the saloons of the Wild West to the salons of Paris, people will always find a reason to get together. It's in our nature.

Poet, novelist, and icon Gertrude Stein hosted the most famous Parisian salon in her home at 27 Rue de Fleurus. That was 100 years ago. The world was fresh out of World War I and still recovering from the Spanish flu pandemic. Life was grim, and the population was shell-shocked. For political and economic reasons, artists and writers of all sorts flocked to Paris. With her partner, Alice B. Toklas, Stein created a respite for these disillusioned souls. They dined, partied, and debated their fiercest passions, coming together in a cymbal-crash of good times and creative ideas. She deemed these revelers the "Lost Generation," but we like to think of them as Party People Precursors (PPP).

The sentiments of that time are eerily similar to today. Many of us are feeling let down, burnt out, and isolated. This isn't something we can combat alone. Coming together despite it all enables us to rebel against the social constructs that put us here. A party creates a liminal space for people to be weird and wild. When done right, it serves as both a chaotic *and* a safe place to allow unfiltered fun. At parties, we *all* get messy sometimes, whether that's talking for a little too long about why you're sure ghosts are real, loudly telling your best friend that they should reconsider dating that dum-dum … while standing next to the dum-dum, or realizing you had one too many glasses of wine and that's why you simply cannot stop dancing. Party People know that we're all in this together. Party People can balance the grace needed to stay soft with the grit required to get rowdy.

They are the ride-or-die folks you always want by your side. Your emergency contacts. The ones with whom you can be real—the people you fight, cry, and laugh with. They know all of your dreams and most of your secrets. Being a Party Person isn't a choice; it's coded in our DNA (see above, re: Neanderthals). Despite the differences that separate us, we all are looking for the same thing, and we can almost always find it across a table strewn with half-cleared dinner plates bathed in the soft glow of candlelight. That thing we are looking for is connection, and we need it now more than ever.

Statistically speaking, the happiest societies are community-centered, where family and friendships come first. We, however, live in an individualistic society. We are taught to base our worth on output and income, and it's not doing us any good. In 2018, Prime Minister Theresa May appointed the UK's first Minister for Loneliness, and in 2023, US Surgeon General Vivek Murthy proclaimed that we are in a loneliness epidemic. According to the Roots of Loneliness Project, loneliness has increased by 181 percent since 2020. That's not a typo—181 percent. Numerous studies have correlated loneliness with increased risks of depression, anxiety, suicide, dementia, and chronic health conditions such as heart disease, hypertension, inflammation, and diabetes. One study went so far as to say the impact of loneliness on mortality is like that of smoking 15 cigarettes a day.

By far, the most prevalent cause of loneliness is feeling disconnected. And no, the internet does *not* count as connection—social media can be devastating to our bodies, brains, and souls. But the answer isn't as simple as meeting a friend for a catch-up over coffee and discussing the weather. Psychologist Carl Jung stated that loneliness does not come from having no people around you but from being unable to communicate the things that seem important to you. We need to feel seen, heard, and understood by those we care about in order to combat loneliness.

One of the best ways to do that is to throw a party. It can be a party of two or 200; it doesn't matter. (In some cases, it can even be a party of one; see page 215.) Whatever the size of your party, we are here to help. Make no mistake, this is a cookbook about entertaining, and our biggest inspiration—besides *The Garfield How to Party Book,* a ridiculous, entertaining guide from the eighties for anyone who hates Mondays and loves lasagna—is the queen of entertaining herself, Martha Stewart. But while we'll never deny our sincere and unadulterated love for her, our version of entertaining is quite different. We like to think of ourselves as Martha's neurodivergent stepkids. Whereas Martha has more than 200 fruit trees growing on her farm, Brie has just one that came with her house. (She did, however, manage to plant a small but mighty herb garden that would make Martha proud.) Courtney, on the other hand, has an Italian parsley plant that she forgot to water, so now there's just a pot of dried-up twigs sitting on her balcony. It's been there for more than a year. But the spirit of Martha remains. She raised us into the women we are today. While Martha was rolling out perfect piecrusts, we were at her feet, gathering up all the dough scraps and using them to make deformed hand pies—still a good thing, but decidedly not perfect. The amount of partially finished crafts you could find at either of our houses would astound you. It's not because we don't care; it's because we care too much. We want to do all the things, but time is of the essence and our attention spans can only take us so far. So let us show you how to entertain the Party People way.

First, you have to laugh in the face of perfection. If you are so focused on your soufflé that you miss the moment your friend opens up about a huge, important thing in their life, then the party is moot. And don't feel like you have to work the whole night just because you are hosting. Let your friends help lighten the load. Have Laura bring the bread. Mo can swing by the store and pick up some extra butter on the way. Where's Gareth? Oh, he's in the kitchen chopping onions like it's his job, because it *is* his job if you have anything to say about it. And who cares if someone messes up? If the soufflé falls because Kate was in the middle of a fantastic story that you just couldn't pull yourself away from, then *great*! If you accidentally make charcoal by forgetting about the sliced zucchini and leaving it on a blazing hot grill overnight, then kudos to you, my friend. (Courtney has actually done this, as evidenced by the photograph to the right. Do not try this at home, kids.)

With this book, we are giving you the tools to spark a new dining revolution in your home, one where connection takes center stage and entertaining is an afterthought. Our goal is to help you get so deep in the moment that you forget to post about it on social media. The things on our phones don't matter, but the people in front of us do. We are in this together, so pour yourself another Scorpion Slush (page 61) and pass the Cheesy Jenga Bread (page 79). This party is just getting started.

Take this quiz to find out:

1 Do you like to have a good time? **YES NO**

2 Do you like to help others have a good time? **YES NO**

3 Have you ever slipped and fallen because you were dancing too hard? **YES NO**

4 Have you ever cooked food just for the fun of it? **YES NO**

5 Have you ever started a craft or art project and never finished it? **YES NO**

6 Have you ever started a craft or art project and finished it? **YES NO**

7 Have you ever received cheers or jeers upon entering or leaving a party? **YES NO**

8 Have you ever worn a lampshade on your head? **YES NO**

9 Do you prefer to hold a conversation without making eye contact? **YES NO**

10 Have you ever been late to a party on purpose because you were nervous? **YES NO**

11 Do you sometimes lie awake at night, wondering if you've made the right decisions for your life's journey, but then realize "Hey man, life *is* the journey" and then immediately fall back asleep? **YES NO**

12 Have you ever uttered any of the following phrases: "You know what this needs? More cheese." I can't believe we actually got away with that!" "Don't worry, there's plenty more in the freezer." **YES NO**

13 Does any part of you enjoy gardening? **YES NO**

14 Have you ever laughed at a joke that wasn't even remotely funny out of sheer social anxiety? **YES NO**

15 Have you ever forgotten someone's name immediately after they told it to you? **YES NO**

16 Do you have a go-to karaoke song? **YES NO**

If you answered yes to one or more of these questions, then congratulations, you are 100 percent a real-deal, bona fide Party Person!

PARTY PERSON ARCHETYPES

Now that we've established that you are, in fact, a Party Person, it's time to meet your peers. We all bring something to the table, and it's our differences that make life interesting. Party People are a vast, dynamic group, and we couldn't possibly include every single archetype here, so these are just a few of our favorites. We've noted everyone's best match, too, so take those into account if you are the type who likes to make seating arrangements.

the party animal

Sometimes the Party Animal gets a bad rap, and for good reason. But imagine how boring parties would be without them. They are the ones who tell the wildest stories. They start a cash pool to get another keg delivered. They turn up the music and are the first ones on the dance floor. You might be cleaning up their vomit later, but it was probably worth it.

Best match: the One with the Interesting Booze.

the one with the interesting booze

Whether it's a funky orange wine from a small vineyard upstate or an IPA micro-brewed in their basement, the One with the Interesting Booze is bringing the good stuff, and they are always down to share.

Best match: the Party Animal.

the party pooper

In the same way that shadows can't exist without light, parties cannot exist without Party Poopers. They complete the circle. With their dry wit and keen observations, they are also a really fun hang, if you can actually convince them to come out.

Best match: the Womp-Womp.

the host with the most

If you're reading this book, then you most likely are the Host with the Most. These are the ultimate Party People. They're the ones who open their hearts and their homes to throw the parties.

Best match: the Helper.

the late one

These folks are always on the way but never quite arriving. Once you recognize a Late One, adjust their call time accordingly. Party starts at 8? Tell them 6 p.m. sharp.

Best match: By the time they get there, it won't really matter.

the helper

Need a hand with the dishes? They are on it. Ran out of ice? They'll pop out and grab some more. Behind every Host with the Most is a Helper. Cue up "Wind Beneath My Wings."

Best match: the Host with the Most.

the shy one

The best thing about a Shy One is that after a couple drinks, they almost always turn into a Party Animal. They will also listen intently to every story told by the Nostalgic One.

Best match: the Nostalgic One.

the topper

They've been there, done that, it's way better than any experience you've ever had, and they sure as hell aren't afraid to tell you about it.

Best match: the Know-It-All.

the know-it-all

Strongly opinionated and up on all the latest reports and indexes, these folks have something to say, and they tend to say it loudly.

Best match: the Topper.

the nostalgic one

Remember that time you acted like a total dip, got kicked out of the bar, and almost got arrested? Of course you do, because the Nostalgic One brings it up at every. single. party.

Best match: the Shy One.

the womp-womp

Also known as an energy vampire, most interactions with a Womp-Womp can be exhausting, but these Party People are deeply misunderstood. They just need to get a few things off their chest and then when that dance floor opens up, they tend to get freaky.

Best match: the Party Pooper.

If you don't see yourself represented here, fill in the blank with your own Party Person archetype, and keep us posted.

?

_____
_____
_____
_____
_____
_____
_____

THE OFFICIAL

Party Person Pledge

I, _____,

do uproariously swear that I will faithfully execute my role of Party Person and cultivate a lifestyle where good times and tasty bites are always on deck. I pledge to welcome all of my fellow Party People to the table to the best of my ability, and above all, I vow to never stop partying.

FOR
PEOPLE
WHO
Party

SIGNATURE
_____

DATE
_____

Brie Larson
PARTY PERSON

Courtney McBroom
PARTY PERSON

Pursuant to subsection 922(FO) of the Statutes of Party People Authority, this document holds binding significance in the court of public party law.

EIGHT STEPS TO THROWING A PARTY
(or How to Use This Book)

You got the book, and you want to throw a party: That much is clear. The problem is you have no clue how to go about doing it. Well, simply follow the eight steps below and you'll be on your way. In fact, you'll be more than on your way, you'll be *at* the party that you threw.

step 1: pick a reason

The more mundane the reason for a party, the better. It's the little things that make a life, and it's time we started celebrating them. Use our examples below, or feel free to come up with your own.

> **You found the perfect pair of jeans!**
>
> **You landed the deal!**
>
> **You finally ended things with that dum-dum!**
>
> **You had a breakthrough in therapy!**
>
> **You nailed the audition!**
>
> **You got a new pet!**
>
> **You either escaped or made jury duty, depending on your preference!**
>
> **Hey, it's Hanukkah!**
>
> **Merry Christmas, ya filthy animal!**
>
> **Thanksgiving cornucopias commence!**
>
> **Sports!**
>
> **You secured the loan!**
>
> **You had a UFO encounter!**
>
> **You did a really hard thing that you thought you couldn't pull off, but you totally pulled it off!**
>
> **Your landlord has decided not to raise rent after all!**
>
> **That weird mole? Not cancer!**
>
> **You survived your first mammogram!**
>
> **You saw a ghost!**
>
> **You discovered a new show to binge!**
>
> **You scored cheap tickets to Bermuda!**
>
> **You woke up today!**
>
> **_____! (Fill in the blank.)**

step 2: set a date and invite your people

You can text, email, or send invites the old-fashioned way, via carrier pigeon. Likely not everyone will be able to attend, and that's okay. Don't *not* throw a party just because one or two of your friends can't make it. Pick a date that works for most. Another option is to have a standing party. It can be weekly, monthly, or even quarterly; it just needs to stay consistent so people can keep it in their calendars. Invite or send a reminder two weeks in advance to get a proper head count.

step 3: pick the vibe

Party People is divided into three parts. The first is Party Essentials, which includes recipes needed for every party, no matter the vibe: libations, party snacks, and sweets. Part 2, aka Let's Party, is where the vibes come in. Within this section, go to the Casual Parties chapter (page 116) for something super laid-back, or, to up the ante, turn to Fancy Parties on page 144. If you'd rather keep it small, turn to page 186 for some Tiny Parties that you and your BFF will love. Within each of the chapters in the Let's Party section are recipes that fit the casual, fancy or tiny vibe. You'll pick a few and then add a libation, some party snacks, and a dessert from part 1 (Party Essentials). If you don't feel like picking any recipes, don't worry: We've provided sample menus and prep plans at the end of each chapter. You are welcome to use those. Part 3 is our theme party section, which is why it's called Theme Parties. It contains stand-alone parties with set menus. One of them may or may not revolve around hot dogs. Go to this section for a one-stop shop.

By the way, all the recipes in this book are great à la carte, too. They are already divvied into classic cookbook recipe categories in the table of contents (page 6), so you can reference them based on the type of food you want, in case you wake up one morning and simply must have Chicken Spaghetti (page 134). Keep in mind that all the serving sizes listed are based on these dishes being part of a full dinner-party menu, so if you are making something à la carte, it might not feed as many people as if you were serving it alongside party snacks, sides, and desserts.

step 4: create the ambiance

A party without ambiance is just a conference with fewer spreadsheets. You gotta create a space where everyone feels comfortable, inspired, and loved—including you. Take the time to make a good playlist or have a trusted friend do it for you. Consider your outfit. It doesn't need to be haute couture, but it should represent the vibe of the party or at the very least your hosting style. Lighting is key; everyone wants to look good, and good lighting is how to do it. Should your schedule and budget allow, break out the decorations. Nothing says *party* like a wall of streamers and a disco ball. Be sure to plan all of this in advance to avoid headaches on the day of your shindig, and check out page 24 for more detailed entertaining tips, because we couldn't possibly fit them all into just this one paragraph.

step 5: get to cooking

Tee yourself up by prepping ahead as much as possible. Many of our recipes can be made in advance, and we've noted them as such. We've also mentioned which ones can be frozen, because a true Party Person always stocks their freezer with things like Party People Pepperoni Pizza Pockets (PPPPP; page 88) for those late-night moments when everyone ends up back at their place requiring snacks. When making things ahead of time, choose storage containers wisely. If a container smells like garlic, it will infuse that flavor into whatever you put inside—definitely not a good place to store cocktails or desserts. The same goes for cutting boards—have one that's just for fruit and sweets, and never cut alliums on it.

Most recipes in this book are written to serve eight people as part of a full menu. This is a great number because it can easily be halved or doubled according to your needs. For a typical party, check out the box to the right, but keep in mind that we do like to err on the side of leftovers, so round up if needed.

Oh, and if a recipe calls for "½ teaspoon chopped fresh parsley," it means you chop the parsley first and then measure out ½ teaspoon. If it says, "1 teaspoon fresh parsley, chopped," you measure out 1 teaspoon of parsley and then chop it. This goes for all measurements across the board. If the action goes before the ingredient, do the action first. If the action goes after the ingredient, measure first and then do the action.

- Two drinks per person during the first hour and then one drink per person for every subsequent hour. This works for any combination of cocktails, beer, wine, or nonalcoholic beverages.

- Three bites per person of Party Snacks (page 66).

- Three ounces (85 g) of meat and cheese per person for a charcuterie board.

Before we move on to step 6, we need to address something important. In our experience, there are three barriers to throwing a party—time, money, and know-how—and we are officially giving you permission to hack the firewall. If you're short on time or lacking in know-how, pick one easy recipe, like The Simplest of Salads (page 166) or the Old Pal (page 52), and supplement it with premade grocery items or takeout. As for money, you won't find beluga caviar or saffron within these pages. But even so, feeding a group can be expensive, so if you need to have an instant-ramen party for budgetary reasons, we support that. These recipes aren't going anywhere; you can make them some other time. The most important thing is that you keep partying. You are a Party Person, after all.

step 6: set the table

Organize this task as much as possible in advance. At least a few hours before the party—or even better, the day before—get out your serving bowls, platters, and utensils, and leave notes on each with the name of the recipe it will be holding. When it comes to individual plates and utensils, go in any direction you want. Wedding china, mismatched vintage, compostable paper—nothing is off the table. Speaking of which, a fun tablecloth, candles, and a floral arrangement, although not necessary, always add a nice touch. The flowers can even be foraged from your backyard or garden. Seating arrangements are a good idea for Fancy Parties (page 144); this forces new encounters and prevents awkwardness from people who don't know where to sit. Should you choose to go this direction, look to the Party Person Archetypes (page 16) for suggestions on who to seat next to whom.

step 7: set the bar

Much of the bar setup can also be done in advance. The beverages in this book are batched out, so all your guests will have to do is shake or stir theirs with ice and then top it off with a mixer, if needed. The slushies (starting on page 60) are a whole different beast, but we'll get into that later. Each bar setup should have the following:

Set these up in advance: cocktail glasses, water glasses, wine glasses (if serving wine), a cocktail shaker (if needed), a stirring spoon (if needed), cocktail napkins, cocktail picks, a jigger, a bottle opener or wine key (if needed), ridiculous crazy straws, tiny paper umbrellas (not optional).

Add these just before your guests arrive: a filled ice bucket and ice tongs, cocktail garnishes, the batched-out cocktail(s), beer and wine (if serving, and on ice, if needed), mixers (if needed), carafes of drinking water (still and sparkling).

Word to the wise: Sometimes home freezers make ice taste weird. If that's the case with yours, buy a bag of ice specifically for cocktails.

step 8: let the party begin

If you followed steps 1 through 7, your party will begin at any moment. Remember to laugh in the face of perfection and take everything in stride so you can actually enjoy the fact that your friend Faye nailed her audition or that Charlie finally scored that perfect pair of swim trunks. As your people arrive, show them to the bar so they can make themselves a drink and have some snacks. If you are still prepping, invite them into the kitchen to hang with you until more guests show up. From there, the night will be what you make of it. Now, go forth and party.

PRACTICAL ENTERTAINING TIPS FOR EVERY PARTY PERSON

As a host, you have a lot of things on your mind, most of them ways to help your guests have a great time. Here are our thoughts on how best to make that happen. Heed what you like, and ignore the rest.

First and foremost, enjoy yourself. Erratic, bad energy is contagious. If you aren't having fun, there's no way any of your guests will. If you need to take a break, pull a Gatsby and excuse yourself to a private area away from the crowd for a few minutes and take some deep breaths.

To shoe or not to shoe? If you are a shoes-off household, it's always nice to inform your guests ahead of time so they can plan accordingly. If you want to up the ante, provide house slippers or funny socks for them at the door. Keep in mind that some attendees (including the elderly) may need to keep their shoes on for anti-slip purposes.

Create a safe zone for those who need it. Set up an activity table. It doesn't have to be a big table, or a big activity, but it will provide big solace for those with social anxiety or for anyone who needs a break from prolonged eye contact with strangers. It also helps people bond in a novel way. They can work on the activity together instead of engaging in boring old small talk. More than one romance has begun this way! Some ideas for activities include a jigsaw puzzle, Jenga, Mad Libs, or Twister. To take it a step further, we recommend a full-blown Game Night (page 140).

Lighting. Bright overhead lighting is a no-no. Candles are far better, and they work wonders for creating a vibe. If you are worried about starting a fire, electric candles are a great option.

Temperature. Keep the thermostat set at something comfortable. If you are the type who keeps your place chilly, offer blankets or sweaters to those who may be adversely affected, or tell them ahead of time to bring a jacket. (Or just keep the thermostat set at something comfortable, like we said the first time.)

Speaking of jackets . . . Unless you are entertaining a large crowd, it's easiest to clear a bed for people to lay their coats and bags on. If there are too many coats to fit on the bed, purchase an inexpensive clothing rack and some extra hangers.

Telephones. Encourage everyone to keep phone use to a minimum. If that doesn't work, it's perfectly fine—nay, encouraged!—to take a shoebox, tell everybody to put their phone in it, and bury it in your backyard.

Music volume. With the exception of a dance or karaoke party, it's best to keep music set at a level that people can hear it *and* the person they are talking to without having to raise their voices. Please note that the Party Animals (see page 16) may turn it up when you aren't paying attention, so keep an eye on them until it's time to hit the dance floor.

Photos. People can, and likely will, take photos with their phones (unless said phones are six feet under in your backyard), but 35mm film cameras are so much fun. Buy the disposable kind, or spend a little extra and get a cool vintage one. However, if you are a private person, it's completely acceptable to enact a "no-photo" policy.

Signage. If you live in a place where the location of the bathroom isn't obvious, slap a cute lil' sign on the wall to point people in the right direction. Same goes for a smoking area or any place that you want people to find easily without having to ask.

Help them help you. Encourage people to help themselves to things like water, beer, and wine from the fridge. This frees you up from constantly having to serve everyone, and it will be a respite for those who don't want to bug you for things.

Dietary restrictions. Ask ahead of time if anyone has a serious food allergy, and if someone does, be sure to accommodate them. They don't need to be able to eat everything that's served, but it's nice to offer a few options. For those with dietary preferences (vegan, vegetarian, hates onions), use your best judgment. If you are having a BBQ Beef Bonanza and invite your vegan friend, give them a proper heads-up and plan to throw a few mushrooms on that griddle before you hit it with the flank steak. If that seems like too much work, it's probably better to invite them to a different party.

Ask for help. There's no such thing as too many cooks in the kitchen. In fact, that's part of the fun! Don't be afraid to ask your people to chop onions, pick herbs, or turn on the grill. Heck, you can even ask them to help clean up.

Lights out. When it's time for everyone to go home, just tell them. You're tired! It's okay.

And now, a few tips for the guests: RSVP in a timely manner. Never ghost the host. Ask if you can bring anything, and if the answer is yes, bring it. Most importantly, don't be a jerk.

PARTY TOOLS AND EQUIPMENT

Beyond the usual stuff like knives (make sure they're sharp), whisks, baking sheets, tongs, mixing bowls, and cutting boards, every serious Party Person must have a few things. Here they are, in no particular order:

8-cup (2 L) high-speed blender

Food processor

Mandoline

Microplane

Fine-mesh sieve and a ladle to help push liquids through it

9 × 13-inch (23 × 33 cm) baking dishes, for sheet cakes and casseroles

Stand mixer or hand mixer

Large Dutch oven

Spider

Large pitcher for mixing batched cocktails

Large storage containers for storing batched cocktails

Thermometers (one for frying, one for meat, and one for the oven)

Pastry brush

Mortar and pestle (not necessary, but oh so much fun)

Slushie machine (absolutely not necessary, but again—so fun!)

Cooling rack

A garden (okay, you don't have to have a garden, but if you can swing it, it would be very Martha of you)

THE PARTY PERSON'S PANTRY

We won't bore you with a long list of ingredients here. If you see one in a recipe, it's there for a reason, so use it. We do need to point out a few logistical things, though.

Get a cheaper **olive oil** for cooking and a fancier one to use raw for things like salad dressings or the Amore Amaro Cake (page 98). In either case, the olive oil should be extra virgin.

All **butter** is unsalted. 2 sticks = ½ pound (227 g) = 1 cup = 16 tablespoons.

They say you can make **buttermilk** from scratch, but it doesn't work the same. Just buy some. We use it enough in this book to justify purchasing the quart (946 ml) container, which is the only size it comes in and is so annoying because who uses that much buttermilk? We do, that's who. Plus, it lasts forever—way past what the expiration date on the package would have you believe.

Black pepper is freshly ground, **milk** is whole, **eggs** are large, **light brown sugar** is packed. **Onions** are medium or about 1½ cups (200 g) chopped.

Always buy blocks of **cheese** and shred them yourself. The pre-shredded kind is coated in a weird anticoagulant that makes it melt funny.

Avoid using packaged, peeled, or pasted **garlic.** Fresh is best.

THIS ONE IS IMPORTANT!!! Our recipes were tested using **Morton's kosher salt.** Not necessarily because we like it better; just because there was a Diamond Crystal shortage going on at the time. Both options are great. Diamond Crystal is less salty, so if you use it, you will need to add about ⅓ teaspoon extra for every 1 teaspoon of Morton's. We also use larger, extra flaky finishing salt from time to time. Our go-to is Maldon; it's a classic for a reason.

We call for pretty much every type of **vinegar.** You can sort of get away with interchanging them, but if you can, use the one called for in the recipe, because there are differences.

If you aren't saving your **bacon** grease, then you are majorly screwing up. Get a container, fill it with the good stuff, store it in the fridge, and use it anytime you want to impart a smoky, porky flavor in a dish. Use it just like you'd use any other cooking oil.

When it comes to **spices and herbs,** we always specify fresh or dried. Dried herbs are more potent, so if you must convert, use a 1:3 ratio of dried to fresh. Dried spices and herbs do lose flavor over time, so replace them every year at least.

Any time you have meat, bones, or veggie scraps like onions, carrots, or celery (avoid cruciferous and starchy, potato-esque vegetables), save them in the freezer. When you have enough stockpiled, use them to make **stock.** Store the finished stock in the freezer until you're ready to use it. It's the circle of life.

We use **cake flour** for many of our cakes. You can sub with all-purpose; the finished cakes will just be a little denser, with a larger crumb.

We call for a lot of **hot sauce** in this book, and we are pretty specific about which kinds. We like to keep a huge array on hand because they all offer different heat levels and flavor profiles. It takes forever for them to go bad, so there's no reason not to stock up.

We are all about that **dried bean** life. Canned can be substituted, but flavor-wise, dried are superior, plus you can save the cooking liquid. It freezes nicely and makes a great base for soups.

Lemon and lime juice should be freshly squeezed. Depending on their size, one lemon or lime yields 1 to 2 ounces (2 to 4 tablespoons) of juice.

Hot dogs are the most important ingredient in every chef's arsenal, and you should always have plenty on hand.

the condiments

We'd be remiss not to tell you about some of our favorite homemade condiments. You'll find these sprinkled throughout many recipes in this book, but they are great to have on hand no matter what. We use the Garlic Toast Crunchies (page 37) like fairy dust, sprinkling them on anything we want to add texture and flavor to, and you'll never catch us without a squeeze bottle of Swayze Sauce (page 42) in the fridge. All of these taste great on a hot dog, too. That was not an accident.

PICKLY THINGS

PICO DE GALLO

GIARDINIERA

CHOW CHOW

CHOW CHOW

makes about 1 quart (960 ml)

This classic Southern sweet pickle relish can be eaten by itself, but it's commonly used to top other dishes. There's no strict recipe for it, because it was originally invented as a way to use up whatever summer vegetables were left at the end of the season. Here's our favorite version.

½ pound (227 g) green cabbage, core removed and chopped into ½-inch (1 cm) pieces (about 2½ cups/180 g)

One 6- to 8-ounce (170 to 227 g) turnip, peeled and diced into ¼-inch (6 mm) pieces (about 1¼ cups/160 g)

1 yellow onion, diced into ¼-inch (6 mm) pieces (about 1 cup/150 g)

1 medium green tomato, cut in half and then sliced into ¼-inch-thick (6 mm) wedges (about 1 cup/120 g)

1 small jalapeño, seeded and finely chopped (about 2 tablespoons)

1½ tablespoons kosher salt

½ cup (120 ml) apple cider vinegar

¼ cup (60 ml) distilled white vinegar

¼ cup plus 1 tablespoon (63 g) sugar

2 whole cloves

1 small cinnamon stick

1 small star anise

¼ teaspoon ground turmeric

1 Combine the cabbage, turnip, onion, tomato, and jalapeño in a large bowl, and mix with the salt. Transfer the mixture to an airtight container and leave it in the fridge to dry-brine overnight (or for at least 12 hours).

2 The next day, remove the veggies from the fridge and transfer them to a colander. Rinse and drain the vegetables and then gently press on them to remove any excess moisture. Set aside.

3 Combine the apple cider vinegar, distilled white vinegar, sugar, and ½ cup (120 ml) water in a small pot. Set over medium-high heat, and bring to a boil.

4 Meanwhile, add the cloves, cinnamon stick, star anise, and turmeric to a quart-sized (1 L) jar or heatproof container with an airtight lid. Add the rinsed veggies to the container.

5 When the vinegar mixture boils, pour it into the jar, over the vegetables, up to the top of the container. You may have a little too much liquid; you don't need to use it all, but make sure the veggies are completely covered. (If for some reason you don't have enough liquid, make a little more.) Put the lid securely on the container, and carefully flip it over and shake it a few times to mix everything together.

6 Store in the fridge for at least 24 hours before using (or, even better, 48 hours).

SPECIAL EQUIPMENT
Heatproof quart-sized (1 L) jar with an airtight lid

PREP AHEAD
Make up to 1 month in advance. Store in an airtight container in the fridge.

USED IN
Beefy Italian Sliders (page 91), Kalua Pork (page 150), We're Hot for Hot Dogs (page 218)

GIARDINIERA

makes 1 quart (512 g)

Giardiniera is the unofficial condiment of the Windy City. For a less-spicy version, substitute a bell pepper for the serranos. We hope we did you proud, Chicago!

½ small head cauliflower, cut into bite-size florets (about 2 cups/200 g)

1 medium carrot, sliced ¼-inch (6 mm) thick (about ¾ cup/90 g)

2 celery ribs, sliced ¼ inch (6 mm) thick on a bias (about ¾ cup/75 g)

3 serrano peppers, sliced ¼ inch (6 mm) thick (about ⅓ cup/35 g)

1 tablespoon plus ¼ teaspoon kosher salt, divided

1 cup (240 ml) distilled white vinegar

½ cup (120 ml) grapeseed or canola oil

½ cup (120 ml) olive oil

2 garlic cloves, thinly sliced

2 teaspoons dried oregano

¼ teaspoon celery seed

¼ teaspoon red pepper flakes (optional)

Freshly ground black pepper

1 Place the cauliflower, carrot, celery, and serranos in a large bowl. Add 1 tablespoon salt, and mix to combine. Transfer the salted vegetables to a quart-sized (1 L) airtight container, cover them with water, and store them in the fridge overnight (or for at least 12 hours) to brine.

2 Drain and rinse the vegetables.

3 Add the vinegar, grapeseed oil, olive oil, garlic, oregano, celery seed, red pepper flakes (if using), the remaining ¼ teaspoon salt, and a few grinds of black pepper to the container that the veggies were in. Secure the lid, and shake vigorously to combine.

4 Pack the vegetables back into the container. Close the lid and shake again to make sure they are completely coated and covered. If you find there is too much dressing, spoon some of it out. If you find there's not enough, mix a little more olive oil and vinegar in a 1:1 ratio, and add it to the jar to fully cover the veggies.

5 Let the giardiniera sit in the fridge for at least 2 days before using.

SPECIAL EQUIPMENT
Quart-sized (1 L) jar

PREP AHEAD
Make up to 1 month in advance. Store in an airtight container in the fridge.

USED IN
Beefy Italian Sliders (page 91), Pasta Salad (page 165), We're Hot for Hot Dogs (page 218)

PICO DE GALLO

makes about 1½ cups (360 g)

We put pico in this section because the lime juice kind of acts like a pickling agent. Consider this a fresh, chunky, pickle-ish salsa. Be sure to use good-quality, ripe tomatoes.

3 Roma or Campari tomatoes, seeded and finely diced (about 1 cup/180 g)

½ yellow onion, finely diced (about ¾ cup/100 g)

1 large jalapeño, seeded and finely diced (about ¼ cup/40 g)

3 tablespoons roughly chopped fresh cilantro

3 tablespoons fresh lime juice

Kosher salt

1 Combine the tomatoes, onion, jalapeño, cilantro, and lime juice in a bowl. Season to taste with salt (½ to 1 teaspoon).

2 Cover in an airtight container and store in the fridge for at least 1 hour before using. The pico will continue to pickle and release juices as it sits, so if you want a fresher flavor, make it closer to the time you'll eat it.

USED IN
Chile con Queso (a Love Story; page 118), King Ranch Casserole (page 130), Salsa Verde Snapper (page 153), Fajitas for Two (page 192), We're Hot for Hot Dogs (page 218), Breakfast Taco Casserole (page 245)

PREP AHEAD
Make up to 3 days in advance. Store in an airtight container in the fridge. It will release water as it sits, so strain as needed.

CRISPY THINGS

CHILE LIME SALT

FRIED CAPERS

GARLIC TOAST CRUNCHIES

FRIZZLED SHALLOTS

CINNAMON TOAST CRUNCHIES

FRIZZLED SHALLOTS

makes about 1½ cups (75 g)

This style of shallot is often used in Southeast Asian cooking. Sprinkle it on salads, steaks, casseroles, or anything you want to lend a fried onion vibe. The leftover oil will be infused with flavor; save it for Tomato Tarts (page 80), or use it as cooking oil or to make salad dressings.

3 large shallots

About 1 cup (240 ml) grapeseed, canola, or vegetable oil (or bacon grease, if you're naughty)

Kosher salt

1. Peel the shallots, and use a mandoline to slice them crosswise into ⅛-inch-thick (1.5 mm) rings.

2. Heat ½ inch (1 cm) of oil in a small pot over medium-high heat. Add a couple shallot slices to the pot. When they begin to sizzle, the oil is ready. Add the rest of the shallots, reduce the heat to low, and cook, stirring occasionally, until golden brown, 35 to 40 minutes. Don't rush this; if you fry them too quickly, they risk becoming bitter. Patience is the name of the game.

3. Place a fine-mesh sieve on top of a heatproof bowl. Pour the shallots into the sieve, reserving the oil in the bowl below. Immediately transfer the shallots to a paper towel–lined baking sheet, and use a spoon to spread them into an even layer. They will be a little sticky and clumped up; that's okay. They will continue to darken and crisp up as they cool.

4. Season the shallots with salt while they're still hot and then let cool.

FREEZABLE

SPECIAL EQUIPMENT
Mandoline, fine-mesh strainer

PREP AHEAD
Make up to 2 weeks in advance. Store the shallots in an airtight container at room temperature and the shallot oil in a separate container in the fridge. Store in the freezer for up to 3 months.

USED IN
Miso Deviled Eggs (page 72), Steakhouse Chopped Salad (page 158), Chilled Tofu with Sesame Spinach (page 196), We're Hot for Hot Dogs (page 218), The Stickiest Wings (page 253)

FRIED CAPERS

makes about ½ cup (25 g)

These briny pops of intense flavor amp up everything. Use nonpareil or other small capers. Definitely do not use caper berries; they will explode in the oil. Speaking of which, the leftover oil tastes great. Save it and use it to cook with.

One 4-ounce (118 ml) jar capers
About 1 cup (240 ml) olive oil

FREEZABLE

PREP AHEAD
Make up to 2 weeks in advance. Store in an airtight container at room temperature or in the freezer for up to 3 months.

USED IN
A Different Tuna Helper (page 129); Party People House Salad (page 161); You Say *Tomato*, We Say *Tonnato* (Page 169); Easy Asparagus with Fried Capers (page 203); We're Hot for Hot Dogs (page 218)

1 Drain and rinse the capers, and spread them onto a paper towel–lined plate or tray. Cover them with another paper towel, and gently press on them to dry. Leave them there until most of the moisture has been soaked up, about 5 minutes.

2 Heat ½ inch (1 cm) of olive oil in a small pot over medium heat. Sacrifice one caper to the pot as a test subject. When it starts to sizzle vigorously, add the remaining capers. Continue frying, stirring occasionally, until the capers are browned and crisp on the edges and start to open up, 5 to 8 minutes. (It takes longer than you think it should, but they'll get there.) Drain the capers onto a paper towel–lined plate.

CHILE LIME SALT

makes about ¾ cup (170 g)

Use this salt to rim cocktail glasses, season meats and vegetables, or, in a nod to the fruit cart vendors of LA, sprinkle it on freshly sliced fruits. Arbol chiles are relatives of the cayenne pepper and have a similar heat profile. Guajillos are the dried form of the mirasol chile. You can play around with different chiles; just be sure to use dried, because the fresh ones contain too much water.

3 dried arbol chiles
1 guajillo chile
½ cup (140 g) coarse sea salt
Zest of 4 limes
2 tablespoons sugar

SPECIAL EQUIPMENT
Food processor

PREP AHEAD
Make up to ∞ years in advance. Store in an airtight container at room temperature.

USED IN
Party People Punch (PPP; page 50), Tex-Mex Martini (page 52), Frozen Margs (aka Margarita Slush; page 63), Salted Margarita Pie (page 109), Salsa Verde Snapper (page 153), We're Hot for Hot Dogs (page 218), Mixed Citrus Palomas (page 241)

1 Remove the stems from the arbol and guajillo chiles, and shake out and discard the seeds. Chop or tear the chiles into about 1-inch (2.5 cm) pieces.

2 Add the chiles to a small skillet, set over medium heat, and toast the chiles, tossing occasionally, until they are fragrant and beginning to brown on the edges, about 3 minutes.

3 Cool for a few minutes and then add them to a food processor along with the salt, lime zest, and sugar. Pulse until the chiles have broken down into small flecks, a little larger than the grains of salt.

TOAST CRUNCHIES

Here we have two crunchy condiments inspired by the two best kinds of toast: garlic and cinnamon. One is savory and the other is sweet, but both follow the same procedure. A white French or Italian loaf works best. You can use stale or fresh bread, and no need to remove the crusts. Don't use a strongly flavored sourdough or rye unless you want your crunchies to taste that way. If you don't have a food processor, a high-powered blender will work.

Garlic Toast Crunchies

makes about 1 cup (110 g)

3 cups (100 g fresh or 80 g stale) sliced or torn 1-inch (2.5 cm) pieces of bread

6 tablespoons unsalted butter, melted

½ teaspoon garlic salt

¼ teaspoon garlic powder

1 garlic clove, grated

1 Preheat the oven to 325°F (165°C). Line a baking sheet with parchment paper.

2 Place the bread pieces in a food processor, and pulse to form about 2 cups (480 ml) of coarse crumbs. Transfer the crumbs to a medium bowl, and add the butter, garlic salt, and garlic powder. Toss until the mixture is evenly combined and the bread-crumbs have soaked up all that butter.

3 Spread the crumbs onto the baking sheet, and toast for about 20 minutes, tossing halfway through, until light golden brown. Remove from the oven and let cool for 2 minutes.

4 Carefully transfer the crumbs to a bowl. Add the garlic, and toss to combine.

5 Return the crumbs to the baking sheet, and toast for another 2 to 3 minutes.

6 Remove from the oven and let cool.

FREEZABLE

SPECIAL EQUIPMENT
Food processor

PREP AHEAD
Make up to 1 month in advance. Store in an airtight container in the fridge for up to 1 month or in the freezer for up to 3 months.

USED IN
Southern Mac 'n' Cheese (page 137), Steakhouse Chopped Salad (page 158), Almost Classic Caesar Salad (page 162), Fun Dip Fries (page 200), Kale Salad (Because Everyone Needs to Know How to Make One; page 204), We're Hot for Hot Dogs (page 218)

Cinnamon Toast Crunchies

makes about 1 cup (110 g)

3 cups (100 g fresh or 80 g stale) sliced or torn 1-inch (2.5 cm) pieces of bread

6 tablespoons unsalted butter, melted

3 tablespoons sugar

1 teaspoon ground cinnamon

¼ teaspoon kosher salt

1 Preheat the oven to 325°F (165°C). Line a baking sheet with parchment paper.

2 Place the bread pieces in a food processor, and pulse to form about 2 cups (480 ml) of coarse crumbs. Transfer the crumbs to a medium bowl, and add the butter, sugar, cinnamon, and salt. Toss until the mixture is evenly combined and the breadcrumbs have soaked up all that butter.

3 Spread the crumbs onto the baking sheet, and toast for about 20 minutes, tossing halfway through, until golden brown.

4 Remove from the oven and let cool.

 FREEZABLE

SPECIAL EQUIPMENT
Food processor

PREP AHEAD
Make up to 1 month in advance. Store in an airtight container in the fridge for up to 1 month or in the freezer for up to 3 months.

USED IN
Fun Dip Fries (page 200), Earl Grey Creamsicle Possets (page 211), We're Hot for Hot Dogs (page 218)

SAUCY THINGS

PEPPERONCINI AIOLI

COMEBACK SAUCE

SWAYZE SAUCE

MISO BUTTER

RAMEN RANCH
DRESSING

RAMEN
RANCH
SEASONING

TONNATO

LIME CRÈME
FRAÎCHE

COMEBACK SAUCE

makes about 1½ cups (340 g)

Here's a Southern staple that will keep you coming back. Think of it as a superior version of McDonald's "special sauce."

1 cup (220 g) mayonnaise

¼ cup (60 g) ketchup

2 tablespoons Louisiana-style hot sauce

1 tablespoon plus 1 teaspoon lemon juice

1 tablespoon plus 1 teaspoon Worcestershire sauce

1 teaspoon garlic powder

1 teaspoon mustard powder

1 teaspoon onion powder

1 teaspoon sweet or hot paprika

Freshly ground black pepper

1 Combine the mayonnaise, ketchup, hot sauce, lemon juice, Worcestershire sauce, garlic powder, mustard powder, onion powder, and paprika in a small bowl.

2 Add a bunch of black pepper, and mix to combine.

PREP AHEAD
Make up to 2 weeks in advance. Store in an airtight container in the fridge.

USED IN
Crispy Comeback Potatoes (page 75), Kalua Pork (page 150), We're Hot for Hot Dogs (page 218)

PEPPERONCINI AIOLI

makes about 1¾ cups (390 g)

If you don't have a food processor, you can make this by hand. Grate the garlic and finely mince the pepperoncini and then stir to combine. For a spicier version, use pickled jalapeños instead of pepperoncini.

1⅓ cups (293 g) mayonnaise

6 large pepperoncini, seeded and roughly chopped (about ½ cup/40 g)

¼ cup (60 ml) pepperoncini juice, from the jar

2 garlic cloves, smashed

1 Add the mayonnaise, pepperoncini, pepperoncini juice, and garlic to a food processor.

2 Process until the garlic and the pepperoncini have broken down and combined. Keep it a little chunky.

SPECIAL EQUIPMENT
Food processor

PREP AHEAD
Make up to 2 weeks in advance. Store in an airtight container in the fridge.

USED IN
Beefy Italian Sliders (page 91), A Roast Beef for Us All (page 149), Kalua Pork (page 150), Doritos Canapés (page 250)

TONNATO

makes about 1 cup (120 g)

This Italian condiment brings the flavor. If you love anchovies, use up to three in this recipe; if you hate anchovies, you can omit them altogether, but try to use at least one, okay? Do it for us. If you use the extra-fancy tuna in the glass jars, you may need to add more olive oil to achieve the right consistency. Start with 1 tablespoon and go from there.

One 5-ounce (142 g) can tuna in olive oil, drained

⅓ cup plus 1 tablespoon (95 ml) olive oil

¼ cup (55 g) mayonnaise

1 tablespoon capers, drained

1 tablespoon lemon juice

1 to 3 anchovy fillets

2 garlic cloves, smashed

Kosher salt and freshly ground black pepper

1 Add the tuna, olive oil, mayonnaise, capers, lemon juice, anchovy fillets, and garlic to a blender and puree until smooth.

2 Season with salt and pepper to taste. Congratulations, you're finished!

SPECIAL EQUIPMENT
Blender

PREP AHEAD
Make up to 3 days in advance. Store in an airtight container in the fridge.

USED IN
Miso Deviled Eggs (page 72); You Say *Tomato*, We Say *Tonnato* (page 169); We're Hot for Hot Dogs (page 218)

LIME CRÈME FRAÎCHE

makes 1 cup (220 g)

Don't spend money on packaged crème fraîche when you can spend money on the ingredients and make it at home. It's incredibly easy, and you'll get more bang for your buck. Plus, we add a hint of lime juice for extra zing. The thickness of your crème fraîche will depend on how long you leave it out and the temperature of your kitchen. The longer you leave it out and the hotter it is, the thicker the sauce will be. It will continue to thicken in the fridge.

1 cup (240 ml) heavy cream

2 tablespoons buttermilk

1½ teaspoons fresh lime juice

Pinch of kosher salt

1 Place the heavy cream and buttermilk in a small container with an airtight lid. Cover and shake vigorously for 30 seconds.

2 Leave the container at room temperature until the crème fraîche thickens to your desired consistency, 12 to 30 hours.

3 Stir in the lime juice and salt.

PREP AHEAD
Make up to 2 weeks in advance. Store in an airtight container in the fridge.

USED IN
Amore Amaro Cake (page 98); Cheese Danish Galette (page 110); Spinach, Artichoke, and Green Olive Dip (page 125); King Ranch Casserole (page 130); A Roast Beef for Us All (page 149); Salsa Verde Snapper (page 153); Fajitas for Two (page 192); Fun Dip Fries (page 200); We're Hot for Hot Dogs (page 218); Hotcakes de Elote a la Doña Esthela (page 242)

MISO BUTTER

makes about 1¼ cups (290 g)

Okay, technically you'd need to melt this for it to be a sauce, but we couldn't exactly put it in the pickly or crispy sections. The miso adds a deep umami richness in any place you'd typically use butter. You can even bake with it.

2 sticks (16 tablespoons) unsalted butter, softened

¼ cup (70 g) white miso paste

1 Add the butter and miso paste to a medium bowl, and mix thoroughly to combine. Ta-daaaaa!

PREP AHEAD
Make up to 3 months in advance. Store in an airtight container in the fridge.

USED IN
Dueling Roast Chickens (page 146), Lemony Miso Butter Beans (page 173), Low-Baked Salmon in Miso Butter (page 195), We're Hot for Hot Dogs (page 218)

SWAYZE SAUCE

makes about 3½ cups (880 g)

This hot sauce/barbecue sauce hybrid takes everything it touches to the next level. It's also wonderful to make in bulk and gift to friends in Patrick Swayze–adorned squeeze bottles. For best results, use classic Heinz ketchup and make this in advance because, much like Swayze himself, it only gets better with age. That's why we named it Swayze Sauce.

One 10.2-ounce (290 g) jar chopped Calabrian chiles

2 Roma tomatoes, cored and quartered

2 large jalapeños, seeded and roughly chopped

2 medium poblanos, seeded and roughly chopped

1 large white onion, quartered

1 bunch fresh cilantro leaves and tender stems, roughly chopped

1½ cups (360 g) ketchup

2 tablespoons distilled white vinegar

1 tablespoon fresh lime juice

1 Place the Calabrian chiles, tomatoes, jalapeños, poblanos, onion, and cilantro in a blender and puree until smooth, scraping down the sides of the blender as needed. Make sure to start with the tomatoes next to the blades; their high water content helps get the mixture going. If that doesn't work, add a couple tablespoons of water.

2 Pass the mixture through a fine-mesh sieve directly into a medium pot. Press on the solids to get out as much of the liquid as possible: You should have 2¾ to 3 cups (660 to 720 ml).

3 Set the pot over medium-high heat, and bring the mixture to a boil. Reduce the heat to medium-low and simmer, stirring occasionally and skimming off any foam that rises to the top, until the mixture has reduced to 2 cups (480 ml), 8 to 10 minutes. Remove from the heat, and let cool for about 10 minutes.

4 Stir in the ketchup, vinegar, and lime juice, and store in the fridge until ready to use. It'll only get better over time.

PREP AHEAD
Make up to 1 month in advance. It actually lasts longer, but for legal reasons, we have to put a time stamp on it. Store in an airtight container in the fridge.

USED IN
A Roast Beef for Us All (page 149), Kalua Pork (page 150), We're Hot for Hot Dogs (page 218), Pork Ribs with Swayze Sauce (page 42)

SPECIAL EQUIPMENT
Fine-mesh sieve, blender

RAMEN RANCH DRESSING
(and Seasoning)

makes about 3 cups (700 g) dressing (and about ¼ cup/30 g seasoning)

Nothing beats ranch dressing. You know it; we know it; everyone knows it. This one is extra special because of the Ramen Ranch Seasoning it contains. For that, we harness the power of instant ramen seasoning packets. Eventually you can experiment with any flavor of seasoning packet you want, but start with the most basic, usually called "soy sauce" or "original," depending on the brand. This will make more than enough seasoning to use in the dressing, so use leftovers like you would any other insanely delicious seasoning: It's great on garlic toast, in guacamole, or even in pasta sauce. (We're looking at you, Fettuccine Rancho Alfredo, page 191.) Save the unused ramen noodles for Party People Mix (PP Mix; page 71).

RAMEN RANCH SEASONING

3 packets instant ramen noodle seasoning (about 3¾ teaspoons/18 g)

2 teaspoons onion powder

2 teaspoons dried chives

2 teaspoons dried parsley

1 teaspoon freshly ground black pepper

1 teaspoon dried dill

1 teaspoon garlic powder

RAMEN RANCH DRESSING

1 cup (240 ml) buttermilk

1 cup (220 g) mayonnaise

1 cup (220 g) sour cream

3 tablespoons Ramen Ranch Seasoning

1 To make the seasoning, add the ramen packets, onion powder, chives, parsley, pepper, dill, and garlic powder to a bowl, and whisk to combine.

2 Grind the mixture in a mortar and pestle, or use a spice grinder for a finer texture.

3 Store in an airtight container at room temperature for up to 6 months.

4 To make the dressing, whisk together the buttermilk, mayonnaise, and sour cream in a medium bowl.

5 Add the Ramen Ranch Seasoning, and whisk to combine.

FREEZABLE

SPECIAL EQUIPMENT
Mortar and pestle

PREP AHEAD
The dressing can be made up to 1 week in advance. Store in an airtight container in the fridge. The seasoning can be made up to 6 months in advance. It can also be frozen, but with such a long shelf life, it's not necessary unless you are going into the Ramen Ranch Seasoning business and need to stockpile. If that's the case, we kindly request a cut. Whether you store it at room temp, in the fridge, or in the freezer, it does tend to clump over time, so throw a desiccant in the container, too.

DRESSING USED IN
Steakhouse Chopped Salad (page 158), We're Hot for Hot Dogs (page 218)

SEASONING USED IN
Party People Mix (PP Mix; page 71), French Onion Ramen Dip (page 121), Dueling Roast Chickens (page 146), Fettuccine Rancho Alfredo (page 191), We're Hot for Hot Dogs (page 218)

party essentials:
basic recipes for any occasion

libations

Every party needs a little something to grease the wheels—just ask the One with the Interesting Booze (see page 16). We've divvied this chapter into three sections: spirit-forward batched cocktails, light and bubbly brews, and knock-you-on-your-ass frozen slushies. For each party you throw from the Let's Party section (starting on page 115), pick one of these as your official drink of the night and supplement with any of the following: beer, wine, hard seltzers, soft beverages, tea, or a simple setup of liquor and basic mixers. Always provide water, too, ideally both flat and sparkling. And feel free to ask friends, (especially if they are Helpers; see page 17) to contribute to the cause; an extra bag of ice or some lemons and limes will go a long way.

Each of the batched recipes should be drunk only by those with the strongest of livers, with the exception of the Party People Punch (PPP; page 50), which can be made without booze. The bubbly recipes are vivacious and celebratory, and they have just a *slightly* lower ABV (alcohol by volume) than their batched brethren, except for the Sparkling Pink Lemonade (page 57), which is alcohol-free. The bases for both batched and bubbly can be made ahead, so all you'll need to do is set them out and let your guests top them off and serve themselves. As far as slushies go, at-home machines exist, thanks to Omar Knedlik, the Dairy Queen franchise owner who accidentally invented them in 1958 when he stored his broken soda machine in the freezer, but all you really need is a blender. These should be frozen in advance and given a quick buzz to slush them up before serving. Store any undrunk slushies in the freezer, and top off your guests as needed. Be warned: They go down real easy and sneak up on ya real quick. We included a virgin recipe in this section, too; go to page 61 to find it.

As always, feel free to ask your friends (perhaps a Helper?) to contribute to the cause—an extra bag of ice or some lemons or limes or a mixer or two will go a long way. And don't forget to provide water—both flat and sparkling.

AVIATION

TEX MEX
MARTINI

BATCHED

OLD PAL

PARTY PEOPLE PUNCH (PPP)

makes sixteen 6-ounce (180 ml) boozed-up drinks or ten 6-ounce nonalcoholic drinks

We knew we needed to put a punch in this cookbook, and when we were trying to figure out what direction to take, Brie said it should be reminiscent of Minute Maid Fruit Punch, her favorite from childhood. Never one to turn down an opportunity for innovation, Courtney agreed, and the experimenting began. Turns out, the only way to get something to taste like Minute Maid Fruit Punch is to put Minute Maid Fruit Punch in it. We souped it up by adding a cornucopia of other juices, too. Freshly squeezed is always best, but it's okay if you just need to open up some store-bought containers and pour. There are a few ways to drink this. You can have it flat, you can add club soda or ginger beer to make it fizzy, and of course, you have the option to spike it with booze.

⅓ cup (67 g) sugar

2 cups (480 ml) guava nectar

2 cups (480 ml) fresh orange juice

1 cup (240 ml) black cherry juice

1 cup (240 ml) fruit punch, preferably Minute Maid

1 cup (240 ml) pineapple juice

½ cup (120 ml) fresh lime juice

Rum, vodka, whiskey, tequila, or gin (optional)

1 lime, sliced into wheels

1 orange, sliced into wheels

FOR SERVING

Chile Lime Salt (page 36)

Lime wedges

Ice

Club soda, ginger beer, or sparkling wine (optional)

1 Combine the sugar with ⅓ cup (80 ml) water in a small pot over medium-high heat. Bring to a boil, and give it a quick stir to make sure the sugar has dissolved. Remove from the heat, and cool to room temperature. Now you have simple syrup—congratulations!

2 Combine the guava nectar, orange juice, black cherry juice, fruit punch, pineapple juice, and lime juice in a large pitcher or container. Add half of the simple syrup, and mix to combine. Taste and add more simple syrup, if needed.

3 If you want to spike the punch, add up to 16 ounces (480 ml) of whichever alcohol you prefer, and stir to combine. Float the lime and orange wheels in the mix (see Note). Cover the pitcher, and store in the fridge for at least 8 hours and up to 3 days.

4 To serve, add the Chile Lime Salt to a small plate. Run lime wedges around the rims of the punch glasses and then dunk the rims in the salt. Fill the glasses with ice, and pour the punch over the ice. If the moment strikes you, top with a little club soda, ginger beer, or sparkling wine for fizz.

NOTE
If you have extra fruit lying around, chop it up and add it to the punch. Melon, strawberries, kiwi—anything goes.

SPECIAL EQUIPMENT
Punch bowl, punch glasses

PREP AHEAD
Make up to 3 days in advance. Cover and store in the fridge.

HACKABLE
Skip step 1 and use ½ cup (120 ml) store-bought simple syrup. Be sure to use standard 1:1 simple syrup (equal parts sugar and water). Use store-bought orange juice.

TEX-MEX MARTINI

makes eight 6-ounce (180 ml) cocktails

If frozen margaritas (see page 63) are the unofficial state drink of Texas, then Mexican martinis are unofficially a close runner-up. They are actually quite similar to a margarita but are less sweet, brinier, and always served up. We call our version a Tex-Mex martini because we add a little cumin to the salt rim. Serve these extra frosty, and don't skimp on the salt.

20 ounces (600 ml) añejo tequila

10 ounces (300 ml) Cointreau

8 ounces (240 ml) fresh lime juice

6 ounces (180 ml) green olive brine, from a jar of green olives

6 ounces (180 ml) fresh orange juice

¼ cup (55 g) Chile Lime Salt (page 36)

¼ teaspoon ground cumin

FOR SERVING

Ice

Lime wedges

Green olives

1 Combine the tequila, Cointreau, lime juice, olive brine, and orange juice in an airtight container, and store in the fridge for at least 2 hours and up to 2 days.

2 Mix the Chile Lime Salt and cumin on a small plate. Run a lime wedge around the rims of the martini glasses to moisten them and then dunk the rims in the salt.

3 Fill a cocktail shaker with ice, and pour in 6 ounces (240 ml) of the martini mix. Shake vigorously, and strain into a martini glass. Garnish with a lime wedge and toothpicked olives. Repeat for the remaining martinis.

FREEZABLE

SPECIAL EQUIPMENT
Cocktail shaker, martini glasses, toothpicks

PREP AHEAD
Make the salt, like, 10 years ago. Make the cocktail mixture up to 2 days in advance and store in the fridge or in the freezer for up to 1 month.

HACKABLE
Use kosher salt in lieu of the Chile Lime Salt. Add the cumin and a pinch or two of chili powder to it, and mix well.

OLD PAL

makes eight 3-ounce (90 ml) cocktails

This vintage cocktail from the 1920s is more or less a boulevardier, except it swaps dry vermouth for sweet. The boulevardier is more or less a Negroni, except it swaps bourbon for gin. Based on this information, feel free to make any of these versions. Whichever combo you use, one thing remains constant: Drunken shenanigans will ensue. Top off the Old Pal with a little club soda to turn it into something we like to call the Old Buddy, Old Pal. Technically, to serve this on the rocks, you should strain the cocktail into a new glass of ice after stirring, but because it's already been chilled, we skip this step for ease.

12 ounces (360 ml) bourbon or rye whiskey

6 ounces (180 ml) Campari

6 ounces (180 ml) dry vermouth

FOR SERVING

Ice

Lemon twists

1 Combine the bourbon, Campari, and vermouth in an airtight container, and store in the fridge or freezer for at least 2 hours and up to infinity.

2 To serve on the rocks, pour 3 ounces (90 ml) into a rocks glass with ice, give 'er a stir, and add a lemon twist.

3 To serve up, stir 3 ounces (90 ml) in a mixing glass filled with ice until fabulously chilled, about 30 seconds, strain into a chilled coupe glass, and add a lemon twist.

FREEZABLE

SPECIAL EQUIPMENT
Mixing glass, fine-mesh strainer, coupe or rocks glasses

PREP AHEAD
There's no reason why you shouldn't always have a batched-out container of this in your fridge or freezer.

AVIATION

makes eight 4-ounce (120 ml) cocktails

This purple-hued delight gets its color from crème de violette, a flowery liqueur made from violets. It's a classic pre-prohibition cocktail that we almost lost forever when crème de violette disappeared from market shelves in the sixties. In 2007, a guy in Minnesota brought the Aviation back from the brink when he began to import Rothman and Winter brand crème de violette from Austria. Nowadays, there are lots of options available, but Rothman and Winter is still the one to use. The Aviation is traditionally served up, but if you prefer to have one on the rocks, we won't stop you. If you do, technically you should strain it into a new glass of ice after stirring, but because it's already been chilled, we skip this step for ease.

16 ounces (480 ml) gin
6 ounces (180 ml) fresh lemon juice
4 ounces (120 ml) maraschino liqueur
2 ounces (60 ml) crème de violette liqueur

FOR SERVING
Ice
Amarena cherries

1 Combine the gin, lemon juice, maraschino liqueur, and crème de violette in an airtight container, and store in the fridge for at least 2 hours and up to 1 week.

2 To serve up, fill a cocktail shaker with ice, add 4 ounces (120 ml) of the mixture, and shake until fabulously chilled, about 30 seconds. Strain into a chilled coupe glass, and garnish with a cherry.

3 To serve on the rocks, fill a rocks glass with ice, and pour 4 ounces (120 ml) of the mixture into the glass. Stir vigorously for about 20 seconds, and add a cherry.

FREEZABLE

SPECIAL EQUIPMENT
Cocktail shaker, coupe or rocks glasses

PREP AHEAD
Make the cocktail mixture up to 1 week in advance and store in the fridge or in the freezer for up to 1 month.

AMARO LAMBRUSCO SPRITZ

SPARKLING PINK LEMONADE

BUBBLY

FRENCH 75

FRENCH 75

makes eight 5-ounce (150 ml) spritzes

The French 75 is named after the French 75 mm field gun from World War I, supposedly because you feel like getting shelled by one after drinking it. Times were tough back then, and the population demanded it. Unfortunately, the times haven't gotten much easier, so there's no reason we should stop drinking these. The classic version uses gin or cognac. We prefer gin, but use whichever you like.

⅓ cup (67 g) sugar
8 ounces (240 ml) gin or cognac
4 ounces (120 ml) fresh lemon juice

FOR SERVING

Ice
One 750 ml bottle champagne or
  prosecco
Lemon twists

1 Combine the sugar with ⅓ cup (80 ml) water in a small pot over medium-high heat. Bring to a boil, and give it a quick stir to make sure the sugar has dissolved. Remove from the heat, and cool to room temperature. Now you have simple syrup—congratulations!

2 Combine the gin, lemon juice, and simple syrup in a large container, and store in the fridge for at least 2 hours and up to 3 days.

3 To serve, fill a cocktail shaker with ice, add 2 ounces (60 ml) of the gin mixture, and shake until fabulously chilled, about 30 seconds. Strain into a champagne flute, and top with about 3 ounces (90 ml) champagne. Garnish with a lemon twist.

FREEZABLE

SPECIAL EQUIPMENT
Cocktail shaker, champagne flutes

PREP AHEAD
Make the gin mixture up to 3 days in advance and store in the fridge or in the freezer for up to 1 month.

HACKABLE
Skip step 1 and use ½ cup (120 ml) store-bought simple syrup. Be sure to use standard 1:1 simple syrup (equal parts sugar and water).

AMARO LAMBRUSCO SPRITZ

makes eight 5-ounce (150 ml) spritzes

Move over Aperol spritz, a new Italian stallion just entered the bar. Here, bittersweet amaro hits the dance floor with fizzy Lambrusco, and they groove the night away. Nardini is our go-to amaro, and it delivers in this recipe. Nonino or Averna would work just as well. Go for something you like, as long as it's not too bitter. Fernet, for example, is not the amaro for this. If you like your spritzes bone-dry, swap out the orange juice for pomegranate.

12 ounces (360 ml) amaro, like Nardini

4 ounces (120 ml) fresh orange juice

FOR SERVING

Ice

One 750 ml bottle dry or off-dry Lambrusco

Orange wedges or twists

1 Combine the amaro and orange juice in a large container, and store in the fridge for at least 2 hours and up to 3 days.

2 To serve, fill a rocks or wine glass with ice, add 2 ounces (60 ml) of the amaro mixture, and stir. Top off with about 3 ounces (90 ml) of Lambrusco, and garnish with an orange wedge or twist.

FREEZABLE

SPECIAL EQUIPMENT

Rocks or wine glasses

PREP AHEAD

Make the amaro mixture up to 3 days in advance and store in the fridge or in the freezer for up to 1 month.

SPARKLING PINK LEMONADE

makes eight 5-ounce (150 ml) spritzes

No need to drink boring, flat, yellow lemonade when you can glam it up via crushed raspberries and a sparkling top. Club soda will make this drink drier, tonic will make it sweeter, and prosecco will make it boozy. Dealer's choice.

6 ounces (170 g) fresh raspberries, plus 8 for serving

¾ cup (150 g) sugar

8 ounces (240 ml) fresh lemon juice

FOR SERVING

Ice

1 liter club soda or tonic water, or 750 ml prosecco

Lemon twists

FREEZABLE

SPECIAL EQUIPMENT

Fine-mesh strainer, rocks or highball glasses

PREP AHEAD

Make the pink lemonade mixture up to 3 days in advance and store in the fridge or in the freezer for up to 1 month.

1 Combine the raspberries and sugar in a small pot. Use a fork to crush the raspberries into the sugar until they are fully broken down and saucy. Stir in ¾ cup (180 ml) water. Set over medium-high heat, bring to a boil, and stir to dissolve the sugar.

2 Remove from the heat. Strain the syrup through a fine-mesh strainer, pressing on the raspberries to extract all of their juice. Let the syrup cool to room temperature.

3 Combine the raspberry syrup and lemon juice in a large container, and store in the fridge for at least 2 hours and up to 3 days.

4 To serve, fill a rocks or highball glass with ice, add 2.5 ounces (75 ml) of the pink lemonade mixture, and stir. Top off with about 3 ounces (90 ml) of the club soda, and garnish with a lemon twist and a whole raspberry.

SLUSHIES

HEMINGWAY DAIQUIRI SLUSH

SCORPION SLUSH

PIMM'S CUP SLUSH

FROZEN MARGS

PIMM'S CUP SLUSH

makes eight 8-ounce (240 ml) slushies

Here we have the quintessential British summertime sporting drink, except frozen. And also without lemonade. And we added ginger ale and gin. So really, it's nothing like the quintessential British summertime sporting drink, and our Scottish recipe tester, Bee, was sure to correct us on that immediately. We can all agree that the best part of a Pimm's cup is the garnishes, though. For best results, err on the side of too many fresh herbs. We love any combination of rosemary, dill, sage, mint, basil, and thyme. Every time someone takes a drink, their nose will sink in and catch a whiff of the luscious bouquet.

½ cup (100 g) sugar
20 ounces (600 ml) ginger ale
16 ounces (480 ml) Pimm's No. 1
6 ounces (180 ml) fresh lemon juice
4 ounces (120 ml) gin

FOR SERVING
Fresh herb sprigs
Cucumber slices
Orange slices
Strawberry slices

1 Combine the sugar with ½ cup (120 ml) water in a small pot over medium-high heat. Bring to a boil and give it a quick stir to make sure the sugar has dissolved. Remove from the heat, and cool to room temperature. Now you have simple syrup—congratulations!

2 Combine the ginger ale, Pimm's, lemon juice, gin, simple syrup, and 12 ounces (360 ml) water in a large container.

3 If using a slushie machine, add the mixture to the machine, slush per the machine's directions, and skip to step 6.

4 If using a blender, transfer the mixture to an airtight container, and freeze at least overnight or up to 1 month.

5 When you're ready to slush, use a spoon or firm spatula to break up the frozen mixture and transfer it to a large blender with at least a 64-ounce (1.8 L) capacity. If you do not have a large enough blender, divide the mixture in half and work in batches. Blend to slushify. Store the mixture in the freezer until ready to serve. If it separates, simply blend it again.

6 Pour into glasses, and garnish with sprigs of your favorite fresh herbs and slices of cucumber, orange, and strawberry.

FREEZABLE

NOTE
Sugar content is extremely important for proper slushing, so don't use a reduced-sugar or sugar-free ginger ale.

SPECIAL EQUIPMENT
Blender or slushie machine

PREP AHEAD
If blending, make the base through step 4 up to a month in advance. If using a slushie machine, make the base in step 2 up to 3 days in advance. Store in an airtight container in the fridge. You can also store the slushed drinks in the freezer for up to 1 month. Stir vigorously with a spoon or blend to re-emulsify before serving.

HACKABLE
Skip step 1 and use ¾ cup (180 ml) store-bought simple syrup. Be sure to use standard 1:1 simple syrup (equal parts sugar and water).

SCORPION SLUSH

makes eight 8-ounce (240 ml) slushies

The Scorpion Bowl is a mid-century tiki drink invented by Trader Vic himself. It's meant to be enjoyed communally from a punch bowl with long straws. Our slushified version can be drunk the same way or divided into separate glasses. Its signature flavor comes from orgeat, a sweet almond syrup with floral notes. Do not skip this ingredient; its sugar content is key to making the slush freeze. It also just tastes good. For an alcohol-free version, omit the rum and brandy, and increase the orange juice by 8 ounces (240 ml) and the lemon juice and orgeat by 3 ounces (90 ml) each. Be sure to use alcohol-free orgeat. If you are using the blender method, you'll freeze the mixture overnight and then add a tiny bit more liquid just before blending to get the mixture going. This keeps you from needing to add ice, which waters down the slush.

32 ounces (960 ml) fresh orange juice

10 ounces (300 ml) light Puerto Rican rum, plus 4 ounces (120 ml) if using the blender method

8 ounces (240 ml) fresh lemon juice

8 ounces (240 ml) orgeat syrup

5 ounces (150 ml) brandy

Amarena cherries with juice, for serving

1 Combine the orange juice, rum, lemon juice, orgeat, and brandy in a large container.

2 If using a slushie machine, add the mixture to the machine, slush per the machine's directions, and skip to step 5.

3 If using a blender, transfer the mixture to an airtight container, and freeze at least overnight or up to 1 month.

4 When you're ready to slush, use a spoon or firm spatula to break up the frozen mixture and transfer it to a large blender with at least a 64-ounce (1.8 L) capacity. If you do not have a large enough blender, divide the mixture in half and work in batches. Add 4 ounces (120 ml) rum (or 2 ounces/60 ml per batch), and blend to slushify. Store the mixture in the freezer until ready to serve. If it separates, simply blend it again.

5 Pour into glasses, drizzle some cherry juice on top, and garnish with a cherry.

FREEZABLE

SPECIAL EQUIPMENT
Blender or slushie machine

PREP AHEAD
If blending, make the base through step 3 up to a month in advance. If using a slushie machine, make the base in step 1 up to 3 days in advance. Store in an airtight container in the fridge. You can also store the slushed drinks in the freezer for up to 1 month. Stir vigorously with a spoon or blend to re-emulsify before serving.

HACKABLE
Use store-bought orange juice.

HEMINGWAY DAIQUIRI SLUSH

makes eight 8-ounce (240 ml) slushies

This slushie was responsible for no less than 14 brutal hangovers the morning after our *Cruising for Murder* murder mystery party (a mystery on the high seas that included no less than three novel dance numbers and a secret gambling ring with bottle service). These stats check out because the original version of this drink has been responsible for countless hangovers on behalf of its namesake, Ernest Hemingway. He'd drink up to a dozen at a time while sidled up to the El Floridita bar in Havana, Cuba. A true Hemingway Daiquiri is 2 ounces (60 ml) rum, 0.75 ounce (22 ml) lime juice, 0.5 ounce (15 ml) grapefruit juice, and 0.5 ounce (15 ml) maraschino liqueur shaken and served up, but a drink with that much booze (classic Hemingway!) won't freeze into a slushie, so we increased the grapefruit juice significantly and added a little extra sugar. If you are using the blender method, you'll freeze the mixture overnight and add a tiny bit more rum just before blending to get the mixture going. This keeps you from needing to add ice, which waters down the slush.

⅓ cup (75 g) light brown sugar, firmly packed

36 ounces (1 L) fresh grapefruit juice

10 ounces (300 ml) white rum, plus 4 ounces (120 ml) if using the blender method

7 ounces (210 ml) maraschino liqueur, like Luxardo

6 ounces (180 ml) fresh lime juice

Lime wheels, for serving

1 Add the brown sugar and ⅓ cup (160 ml) water to a small pot, set over medium-high heat, and bring to a boil, stirring to dissolve the sugar and make a syrup. Remove from the heat and set aside to cool to room temperature.

2 Combine the grapefruit juice, rum, maraschino liqueur, lime juice, and brown sugar syrup in a large container.

3 If using a slushie machine, add the mixture to the machine, slush per the machine's directions, and skip to step 6.

4 If using a blender, transfer the mixture to an airtight container, and freeze at least overnight or up to 1 month.

5 When you're ready to slush, use a spoon or firm spatula to break up the frozen mixture and transfer it to a large blender with at least a 64-ounce (1.9 L) capacity. If you do not have a large enough blender, divide the mixture in half and work in batches. Add 4 ounces (120 ml) rum (or 2 ounces/60 ml per batch), and blend to slushify. Store the mixture in the freezer until ready to serve. If it separates, simply blend it again.

6 Pour into glasses, and garnish with lime wheels.

FREEZABLE

SPECIAL EQUIPMENT
Blender or slushie machine

PREP AHEAD
If blending, make the base through step 4 up to a month in advance. If using a slushie machine, make the base through step 2 up to 3 days in advance. Store in an airtight container in the fridge. You can also store the slushed drinks in the freezer for up to 1 month. Stir vigorously with a spoon or blend to re-emulsify before serving.

HACKABLE
Use store-bought grapefruit juice.

FROZEN MARGS
(aka Margarita Slush)

makes eight 8-ounce (240 ml) slushies

Mariano Martinez invented the frozen margarita in Dallas, Texas, in 1971, creating what is now the unofficial drink of the state. As a native Texan, Courtney has been perfecting hers since she could operate a blender. This is her latest, and best, iteration. If you are using the blender method, you'll freeze the mixture overnight before blending. This keeps you from needing to add ice, which waters down the slush.

½ cup (100 g) sugar
14 ounces (420 ml) fresh lime juice
14 ounces (420 ml) tequila blanco
7 ounces (210 ml) Cointreau

FOR SERVING
Chile Lime Salt (page 36)
Lime wedges

1   Add the sugar and ⅔ cup (160 ml) water to a small pot, set over medium-high heat, and bring to a boil, stirring to dissolve the sugar. Remove from the heat, and set aside to cool to room temperature. Now you have simple syrup— congratulations!

2   Combine the simple syrup, lime juice, tequila, Cointreau, and 3 additional cups (720 ml) water in a large container.

3   If using a slushie machine, add the mixture to the machine, slush per the machine's directions, and skip to step 6.

4   If using a blender, transfer the mixture to an airtight container, and freeze at least overnight or up to 1 month.

5   When you're ready to slush, use a spoon or firm spatula to break up the frozen mixture and transfer it to a large blender with at least a 64-ounce (1.8 L) capacity. If you do not have a large enough blender, divide the mixture in half and work in batches. Blend to slushify. Store the mixture in the freezer until ready to serve. If it separates, simply blend it again.

6   Add the Chile Lime Salt to a small plate. Run a lime wedge around the rims of your margarita glasses to moisten them and then dunk the rims in the salt.

7   Pour the slush into the margarita glasses, and garnish with lime wedges.

FREEZABLE

SPECIAL EQUIPMENT
Blender or slushie machine

PREP AHEAD
If blending, make the base through step 4 up to a month in advance. If using a slushie machine, make the base through step 2 up to 3 days in advance. Store in an airtight container in the fridge. You can also store the slushed drinks in the freezer for up to 1 month. Stir vigorously with a spoon or blend to re-emulsify before serving.

HACKABLE
Skip step 1 and use 1 cup (240 ml) store-bought simple syrup. Be sure to use standard 1:1 simple syrup (equal parts sugar and water).

Super Extra Bonus Fun-Time Recipe:
PIÑA COLADA JELL-O SHOTS

makes 24 shots

There is absolutely no way we'd publish this book without including a silly recipe for JELL-O shots. If you like piña coladas, then you've come to the right place. If you like making love at midnight in the dunes of the cape and/or getting caught in the rain, then you've probably still come to the right place. As an added bonus, these shots aren't packed to the gills with alcohol, so you can have a couple without getting so smashed that you end up taking out a personal ad to find your true love and secretly meet them at a bar, only to discover they were sleeping right there next to you all along.

6 clementines or small mandarin oranges

3 ounces (90 ml) pineapple juice, chilled

One 0.25-ounce (7 g) envelope powdered gelatin (2½ teaspoons)

3 ounces (90 ml) Coco Lopez

3 ounces (90 ml) Puerto Rican rum

1 Cut the clementines in half lengthwise (through the poles). Use a small knife to cut around the perimeter of each halved clementine between the fruit and the rind, and use a spoon to scoop the fruit out of the rind. Squeeze the juice from the fruit, measure out ½ cup (120 ml), and set aside. Save any leftover juice for breakfast tomorrow—you'll need it because you're gonna be hungover. Nestle each halved clementine carcass into the opening of an egg container for stability, and set aside.

2 Pour the pineapple juice into a small pot, sprinkle the gelatin on top, and let it sit for about 2 minutes to bloom. The surface of the liquid will look wrinkly, and the gelatin will turn from a white powder into a transparent goo.

3 Set the pot over medium heat, and warm the juice, stirring often, just until the gelatin dissolves, about 1 minute. Don't let it boil.

4 Add the Coco Lopez, rum, and the ½ cup (120 ml) clementine juice, and stir to combine. Pour the mixture into the clementine halves and refrigerate until set, 2 to 3 hours.

5 Use kitchen shears to trim any excess peel from the edges and then use a hot knife to cut each clementine half in half again to make wedges. (Run the knife under hot water to warm it.)

SPECIAL EQUIPMENT
Empty egg tray

PREP AHEAD
Make these up to 4 days in advance. Wrap with plastic wrap or store in an airtight container in the fridge.

party snacks

The French call it "apéro," Americans call it "happy hour," and the Italians and Spanish call it "aperitivo." Whatever you call it, no predinner gathering would be complete without party snacks. (If you happen to be a Know-It-All [see page 16], then you are already aware of all of these terms, and we are so sorry we wasted your time.) The tasty nibbles within this chapter are meant to be eaten as soon as your guests arrive, as a supplement to the rest of your menu. Pick one or two, and serve them alongside your chosen libation (starting on page 46). These are listed in order from lightest to heaviest, so keep that in mind when mapping out your menu. It's best to choose something light to go along with a heavier option. Alternately, you could make a full menu of party snacks alone. You'll need about four of them, including a heavy hitter, to properly feed a crew of eight. On top of the recipes you see here, it's also a good idea to have a couple low-lift things, like mixed nuts, potato chips, or charcuterie, lying around for people to graze on when they first arrive.

SLOW-ROASTED OLIVES

serves 6 to 8 as a party snack

Most people stuff their olives with anchovies. We are not most people; we are Party People, which is why we paste the anchovies with tons of garlic first and then coat the olives in the mixture. The result is an umami blast straight to the kisser. Be sure to use high-quality olives. The best ones are almost always found in the self-serve olive bar section of the grocery store. Go for a mix of colors and brininess for best results.

3 anchovy fillets in oil

3 garlic cloves

¼ cup (60 ml) olive oil

2 teaspoons finely grated lemon zest
  (from 2 large lemons)

4 cups (600 g) unpitted mixed olives

8 fresh thyme sprigs (or rosemary,
  oregano, or any combination of herbs)

1 Preheat the oven to 300°F (150°C).

2 Add the anchovies and garlic to a mortar, and use a pestle to smash them into a paste. You can also hand chop them together on a cutting board, using the flat side of your knife to smash and drag the mixture to help turn it into a paste.

3 Whisk together the anchovy mixture, olive oil, and lemon zest in a large bowl. Add the olives and thyme, and toss until the olives are well coated.

4 Spread the olives on a large, rimmed baking sheet, and bake for 35 to 50 minutes, until they just start to shrivel and become wildly fragrant. Give the pan a shake halfway through cooking.

5 Serve these warm, at room temp, or slightly chilled, and don't forget to put out a little bowl for the pits!

SPECIAL EQUIPMENT
Mortar and pestle

PREP AHEAD
Make up to 1 week in advance.

PARTY PEOPLE MIX (PP MIX)

serves 8 to 10 as a party snack

We can't very well make a party cookbook without a killer recipe for party mix. In ours, we forgo the typical Chex cereal for popcorn, Frosted Flakes, and oyster crackers. The Frosted Flakes bring a soupçon of sweetness that balances the savoriness of the other ingredients, kind of like when you eat caramel and cheese popcorn together. Speaking of which, the popcorn will cook down significantly as it bakes; don't be fooled by the huge amount we call for. It can be freshly popped or pre-bagged like SkinnyPop; just be sure it's not flavored.

8 cups (80 g) popcorn

2 cups (100 g) Frosted Flakes cereal

One 3-ounce (85 g) package dried ramen noodles, crushed into bite-size bits

1 cup (60 g) oyster crackers

1 cup (50 g) Snyder's of Hanover Butter Snaps pretzels, crushed roughly into halves

½ cup (70 g) unroasted cashews

1½ sticks (12 tablespoons) unsalted butter, melted

3 tablespoons Ramen Ranch Seasoning (page 43)

1 tablespoon Worcestershire sauce

1 Preheat the oven to 250°F (120°C). Line two rimmed baking sheets with parchment paper.

2 Combine the popcorn, Frosted Flakes, ramen noodles, oyster crackers, pretzels, and cashews in a large bowl.

3 Combine the butter with the Ramen Ranch Seasoning and Worcestershire sauce in a small bowl. Pour the butter mixture into the dry mix, and toss until evenly coated.

4 Divide the mix between the baking sheets, and spread into a single, even layer. Bake for about 1 hour, until browned and crisp, tossing halfway through cooking and then tossing every 15 minutes after that.

5 Store in an airtight container in the fridge for up to 1 month.

FREEZABLE

PREP AHEAD
Make up to 1 month in advance. Store in an airtight container in the fridge or freezer for optimal freshness.

MISO DEVILED EGGS

serves 8 to 10 as a party snack

After tasting these during round one of recipe testing, our friend Mo, who just so happens to be a deviled egg connoisseur, proclaimed these "the best deviled eggs I've ever had." And they've only gotten better in subsequent recipe testing rounds. The Tonnato and Frizzled Shallots are the trick; they're what separates this recipe from all the other gajillion deviled egg recipes out there.

12 eggs

¼ cup plus 2 tablespoons (82 g) mayonnaise

3 teaspoons white miso paste

3 tablespoons rice wine vinegar

2 teaspoons spicy Dijon mustard

½ teaspoon soy sauce

Kosher salt (optional)

About ½ cup (60 g) Tonnato (page 41)

Frizzled Shallots (page 35)

Fancy olive oil and flaky salt, for serving (optional)

1 Fill a medium pot half full with water, set over high heat, and bring to a boil. Gently place the eggs in the water, and cook them for 10 minutes. Set a timer; this needs to be exact. Drain the eggs and run them under cold water until they are cool enough to handle.

2 Meanwhile, whisk together the mayonnaise, miso paste, vinegar, mustard, and soy sauce in a small bowl. Set aside.

3 Peel the eggs, pat them dry with a paper towel, and halve them lengthwise. Scoop the yolks into a blender or food processor. Add the miso-mayonnaise mixture, and blend until smooth. Season with salt if you want, but you probably won't want to. Add the filling to a zipper-top bag or piping bag, and stash it in the fridge for 30 minutes.

4 Use a paper towel to pat dry the egg whites and clean the edges of any errant yolk. Arrange the egg whites on a platter (one of those cool deviled egg trays would be even better). Loosely cover them with plastic wrap, and pop them in the fridge until the 30 minutes for the filling is up.

5 Snip a tiny corner off the zipper-top bag, and pipe the filling into the egg cavities. Top each egg with a smear of Tonnato and some Frizzled Shallots. Drizzle some fancy olive oil on top, if you wanna. They probably won't need salt, but if you want more, sprinkle some flaky salt on top before serving.

SPECIAL EQUIPMENT

Zipper-top or piping bag, blender or food processor

PREP AHEAD

Make the eggs through step 4 a day in advance. Wrap well with plastic wrap, and store in the fridge. Finish with step 5 just before serving.

CRISPY COMEBACK POTATOES

serves 8 as a party snack

This is a classic roasted potato with tons of garlic that is absolutely delish, but don't take it from us; take it from our extremely talented recipe tester, Bee. She is British, and she knows her way around a *roastie.* (That's the British term for "roasted potatoes.") Needless to say, this recipe is 100 percent Bee approved. To serve them as a party snack, we like to pile up the potatoes on a platter with those toothpicks that look like swords, but they also double as a killer side dish to complement any meal. We like fluffy russets best, but you can use Yukon Golds if you prefer a denser and slightly more buttery tater. When you toss the boiled potatoes with the olive oil, it's okay, encouraged even, for them to break down a little bit. Those mushy, sludgy bits will crisp up in the oven and become the most coveted bites.

4 pounds (1.8 kg) russet potatoes

Kosher salt

¾ cup (180 ml) olive oil

2 garlic cloves, grated

1 tablespoon roughly chopped fresh parsley

Juice of ½ lemon

Comeback Sauce (page 40), for serving

1 Preheat the oven to 425°F (215°C).

2 Peel the potatoes and cut them into 2-inch (5 cm) chunks. Place them in a large pot, and cover with water by about 1 inch (2.5 cm). Set over medium-high heat, and bring to a boil. Season liberally with salt, and reduce the heat to a simmer. Cook the potatoes until you can easily insert a knife into one of them, about 15 minutes.

3 Drain the potatoes and return them to the pot over low heat until all the excess moisture has evaporated, about 1 minute. Add the olive oil, season generously with salt yet again, and toss to combine.

4 Spread the potatoes, including any broken-down bits, on a baking sheet in a single, even layer. (Depending on the size of your sheet, you may need to use two to fit all the potatoes.) Roast in the oven for 40 to 60 minutes, until browned and crispy, tossing and shaking halfway through cooking. The potatoes may stick to the pan at first; if that's the case, use a flexible metal spatula to unstick them and shake them around a bit.

5 Transfer the potatoes to a large bowl. Add the garlic, parsley, and lemon juice, and toss until evenly combined. The garlic will be a little clumpy at first, but keep tossing and it will eventually loosen up, we promise. Serve with the Comeback Sauce on the side.

FREEZABLE

PREP AHEAD
The potatoes can be made ahead through step 4. Store in an airtight container in the fridge for up to 3 days or in the freezer for up to 1 month. Re-crisp in a 425°F (215°C) oven until heated through, about 10 minutes, and then proceed with step 5.

PARTY PEOPLE'S PEACHES, PROSCIUTTO, AND PECORINO PLATTER (PPPP&PP)

serves 8 as a party snack

Here's our spin on the prosciutto-wrapped melon appetizer that we all know and love. We use ripe, juicy peaches instead, and it's even better, in our humble opinion. The only problem is that you have to make this in the summer, when peaches are in season. But don't worry, we have a solve: Sub in pears, persimmons, or papayas when peaches aren't around. (The fruit *must* start with a P to keep the PPPP&PP acronym intact, or this recipe simply will not work.)

3 ripe peaches, halved and pitted

¼ pound (113 g) prosciutto, thinly sliced

1 ounce (28 g) best-quality pecorino

A bottle of the best balsamic vinegar you've got (the thicker, the better)

Handful of fresh basil leaves, torn

1 Cut each peach into 8 equal wedges and set aside. Cut each slice of prosciutto in half lengthwise. Wrap a piece of prosciutto around each peach. If the prosciutto tears or is too small to wrap fully around the peach, fake it till you make it and simply drape the prosciutto over the peach slice instead. Arrange the proscuitto'd peaches on a large platter.

2 Use a peeler to shave a strip of pecorino on top of each peach, drizzle with the balsamic vinegar, and sprinkle with the torn basil. Serve immediately.

PREP AHEAD

This needs to be done à la minute. (Sorry!)

CHEESY JENGA BREAD

serves 8 to 10 as a party snack

This is based on Brie's great grandma's recipe, which has been passed down for generations. Our recipe adds shredded mozzarella, because when it comes to dairy products, we like to go hard. As far as cheese spread goes, Brie's great grandma used Kraft Old English Spread. We tested ours with that, as well as garlic and herb cheese spread from Whole Foods. You can go as highbrow or lowbrow as you want; the most important thing is that the cheese is spreadable, because you are about to slice a loaf of bread into a bunch of cubes and spackle it back together using the spread as mortar. Be generous with the spread but not so heavy-handed that it gets sloppy. Be sure the loaf of bread is large—it should be both tall and wide, about 10 inches (25 cm) long and 6 inches (15 cm) wide (so a baguette is too skinny to work)—and not presliced. Much like learning the rules to a new card game, it's best to dive in and learn this recipe as you go.

One 9-ounce (255 g) container cheese spread, like Kraft Old English Spread or garlic and herb

8 ounces (227 g) shredded low-moisture mozzarella (about 2 cups)

2 sticks (16 tablespoons) unsalted butter, softened

2 garlic cloves, minced

½ teaspoon garlic salt

1 large loaf unsliced white bread

Poppy seeds (optional)

FREEZABLE

NOTE
Don't attempt to slice all the bread at first. It's easiest to slice and spackle as you go because the cheese spread acts as glue and keeps the loaf from falling apart as you continue to dice it up.

PREP AHEAD
This bread can be made up to 4 days in advance, wrapped tightly in plastic wrap, and stored in the fridge, or it can be frozen for up to 1 month. Bake from frozen, covered in foil until warm throughout. Remove the foil, for the final few minutes of baking, until the edges are nice and crispy.

1 Preheat the oven to 350°F (180°C). Line a baking sheet with foil.

2 Use a spatula to stir together the cheese spread, mozzarella, butter, garlic, and garlic salt in a medium bowl until smooth.

3 Use a serrated knife to cut the crust off the bread—top, sides, bottom, the whole shebang. Place the bread on the baking sheet so the longest side is facing you.

4 Now we slice and spackle. From the side that is facing you, cut the bread lengthwise into three equal layers, essentially turning the loaf into three "sheets" of bread with a top, middle, and bottom layer. Starting with the bottom layer, spread about a ⅛-inch-thick (3 mm) layer of the cheese mixture onto the upward-facing side of the bread and then add the middle layer on top. Spread the cheese mixture onto the top of the middle layer and then add the top layer on top.

5 From the top down, slice the bread lengthwise into thirds. This will leave you with three long strips of bread in three layers, for a total of nine strips. Spread the cheese in between the strips. It doesn't matter where you start—just keep spackling as you go. You are a bread mason now!

6 Next, slice crosswise from the top down. Start by slicing the loaf in half, right down the middle. Then spackle it back together. Slice the left side in half, and spackle that back together. Slice each of those halves in half, and spackle. Repeat this on the right side for a grand total of seven crosswise cuts (one in the middle and three on each side).

7 Spackle the remaining cheese mixture over the tops and sides of the bread to seal it all in, and sprinkle the top with poppy seeds (if using).

8 Bake the loaf for 15 to 20 minutes, until golden brown and melty. Serve hot.

DIRECTIONS FOR SLICING THE BREAD

Sideways

Top

Sideways

TOMATO TARTS

serves 6 to 8 as a party snack

This simple, crowd-pleasing stunner yields the prettiest results when different-color heirloom tomatoes are used. When Brie makes it, she passes around a hunk of Parmesan and a cheese grater so everyone can top their tarts with as much cheese as they like. If you happen to have leftover shallot oil and Frizzled Shallots (page 35), skip making the garlic oil in step 2; then, in step 6, brush the tomatoes and pastry border with the shallot oil, and top with Frizzled Shallots in step 8. As an added boon, these tarts can be made vegan by using dairy-free puff pastry and omitting the cheese.

3 tablespoons olive oil

2 garlic cloves, finely chopped

1¾ pounds (800 g) firm, multicolored tomatoes (about 4 medium), sliced crosswise into ¼-inch-thick (6 mm) slices

Kosher salt

All-purpose flour, for dusting

1 sheet puff pastry (about 14 ounces/ 397 g), thawed

Freshly ground black pepper

¼ cup (55 g) pesto

¼ cup (55 g) fresh ricotta

Fresh torn basil and a big ol' hunk of really good Parmesan, for serving

1 Preheat the oven to 400°F (200°C). Line one large baking sheet with a layer of paper towels. Line another baking sheet with parchment paper and then lightly dust the parchment with flour. Set aside.

2 Heat the olive oil and garlic in a small pot over low heat until the garlic just starts to sizzle. Continue to cook until the scent of wafting garlic tickles your nose, about 30 seconds. Don't let the garlic brown. Remove from the heat, and let the garlic sit in the oil to infuse while you finish the tart.

3 Season the tomatoes with salt on both sides and then place them in an even layer on the paper towel–lined baking sheet. Top with another layer of paper towels, and let them sit for 10 to 15 minutes to release their moisture.

4 Roll or stretch the puff pastry on the parchment paper–lined baking sheet into a 9 × 14-inch (23 × 35 cm) rectangle. Use a knife to lightly score a ½-inch (1 cm) border around the edge; don't cut all the way through the pastry. Prick the inside of the puff pastry with a fork every couple inches.

5 Pat the tomatoes dry and arrange them on top of the puff pastry, within the border, in a pretty design of colors and sizes, overlapping the slices slightly.

6 Strain the garlic from the oil, and set aside the garlic. Brush the tops of the tomatoes and the pastry border with the oil, and sprinkle with black pepper.

7 Bake for 30 to 35 minutes, until the pastry is puffed and golden.

8 Cut the tart into small, appetizer-size squares. Drizzle each square with some pesto and dollops of fresh ricotta and then top with the basil and reserved garlic. Serve warm or at room temperature, with the hunk of Parmesan and a cheese grater on the side to allow your guests to cheese their tarts as much as they want.

PREP AHEAD

This tart can be made a couple hours in advance and left at room temperature, loosely wrapped in plastic wrap.

CALIFORNIA "HAND ROLLS"

serves 8 as a party snack

These aren't true hand rolls because we forgo sushi rice. If you'd like to bulk them up, you can totally serve them with rice, but we prefer to keep them light, because this is technically a predinner snack. Use imitation or canned crab and any flavor of roasted seaweed you want (we like wasabi). The crab mixture can be made in advance, but the avocados and cucumbers should be sliced just before serving. Japanese Kewpie mayonnaise is creamier and more umami-forward than American brands because it contains MSG and uses egg yolks instead of whole eggs. That's why we use it here.

1 pound (454 g) imitation or real crab meat

½ cup (110 g) Kewpie mayonnaise

3 teaspoons soy sauce, plus more for serving

1½ teaspoons wasabi, plus more for serving

2 large avocados, peeled, pitted, and thinly sliced

1 English cucumber, cut into ¼-inch-thick (6 mm) matchsticks

Six 0.35-ounce (10 g) packages roasted seaweed snack sheets, any flavor

Toasted sesame seeds

1 Combine the crab meat, mayo, soy sauce, and wasabi in a medium bowl. Cover and store in the fridge for up to 4 hours.

2 To serve, arrange the avocado, cucumber, seaweed sheets, and sesame seeds on a platter, next to the bowl of crab. The name of the game is for everyone to make their own hand rolls by spooning the crab filling onto a seaweed sheet; topping it with avocado, cucumber, and sesame seeds; folding it up; and popping it in their mouth. Serve with extra soy sauce and wasabi on the side.

PREP AHEAD
The crab mixture can be made up to 4 hours ahead.

PARTY PEOPLE PEÑO POPPERS (PPPP)

serves 6 to 8 as a party snack

These aren't deep-fried, fast-casual–restaurant jalapeño poppers. Nooooo, these are much better. Stuffed with chorizo, cheese, and a little corn for some elote vibes, these bacon-wrapped poppers are more likely to be served in a cute little mom-and-pop spot than your neighborhood TGI Fridays. They are also a staple at Courtney's dad's house. He likes to throw them on the grill. Word to the wise: Don't touch your eyeballs or nether regions for a few hours after prepping all those jalapeños.

¼ pound (113 g) ground chorizo

6 ounces (170 g) cream cheese, softened

2 ounces (55 g) cheddar, grated (about ½ cup)

1 ear fresh corn, kernels cut off the cob (about 1 cup/130 g of kernels)

Kosher salt

10 large jalapeños

10 slices thin-cut bacon, cut in half crosswise

1 Preheat the oven to 400°F (200°C). Line a baking sheet with parchment paper.

2 Cook the chorizo in a medium skillet over medium-high heat until browned, about 5 minutes. Set aside and let cool.

3 Meanwhile, mix the cream cheese and cheddar in a medium bowl. Add the corn kernels and the cooled chorizo, and mix to combine. Season with salt to taste, and set aside.

4 Cut each jalapeño in half lengthwise, including the stems, and use a spoon to scoop out the seeds. Season the insides lightly with salt, and fill each cavity with 1 to 1½ tablespoons of the cream cheese filling. Wrap a slice of bacon around each jalapeño half, being sure to tuck the ends of the bacon underneath the bottom side of the pepper. (This will help keep the bacon in place while baking.)

5 Transfer the assembled jalapeños to the prepared baking sheet, and bake for 15 to 20 minutes, until the bacon is crisp and the filling browns. Let cool for a few minutes before serving.

FREEZABLE

PREP AHEAD
The jalapeños can be prepared through step 4 and stored in the fridge, tightly wrapped in plastic wrap, for up to 24 hours in advance, or frozen for up to 1 month. Bake from frozen.

HACKABLE
Use frozen corn kernels.

COCONUT SHRIMP TOASTS

serves 8 as a party snack

This is a mash-up of deep-fried coconut shrimp and shrimp toast, the classic dim sum dish. Instead of the typical deep-fry, we give these a bath in shallow oil, making them much easier to prep and to clean up. If you don't want to make the sweet and sour sauce from scratch, it's perfectly acceptable to buy some premade from the store.

SWEET AND SOUR STRAWBERRY SAUCE

4 ounces (113 g) fresh strawberries, hulled (about 1 cup)

¼ cup (60 ml) rice wine vinegar

2 tablespoons light brown sugar, plus more as needed

1 teaspoon sambal, or your preferred chili paste (optional)

1 teaspoon soy sauce

⅛ teaspoon kosher salt

1¼ teaspoons cornstarch

COCONUT SHRIMP TOASTS

¾ pound (340 g) shrimp, peeled and deveined

1 egg white

1 small scallion, thinly sliced (green part only)

3 garlic cloves, grated

¾ teaspoon sesame oil

¼ teaspoon kosher salt

Canola or vegetable oil, for frying

6 slices white sandwich bread, crusts removed and each cut into 4 triangles

1½ cups (120 g) sweetened shredded coconut

1 Prepare the sweet and sour strawberry sauce: Add the strawberries, vinegar, brown sugar, sambal (if using), soy sauce, and salt to a blender, and blend until smooth. Transfer to a small pot.

2 Dissolve the cornstarch in 1 teaspoon of water in a small bowl to make a slurry, and stir it into the pot. Set the pot over medium-high heat, and cook the mixture, stirring often, until it begins to bubble. Reduce the heat to a simmer and cook for an additional 30 seconds to activate the cornstarch. Remove from the heat, and let the mixture cool for a few minutes. Taste and season with more salt, if needed, and add more brown sugar, if desired. (Not too much, you sweet-toothed son of a gun!) Store in an airtight container in the fridge for up to 4 days.

3 Prepare the coconut shrimp toasts: Chop the shrimp until they are mostly finely minced but still retain some chunkiness.

4 Mix the chopped shrimp, egg white, scallion, garlic, sesame oil, and salt in a medium bowl.

5 To test the mixture for seasoning, add a splash of oil to a small pan over medium heat. Add 1 teaspoon of the shrimp filling, cook for about 1 minute, until cooked through, and then taste for seasoning. Season the raw mixture with more salt, if needed.

6 Spread about 2 teaspoons of the shrimp mixture on each piece of triangle toast.

7 Add the coconut to a large plate or bowl, and dip each toast, shrimp side down, into the coconut to cover completely.

8 Heat ¼ inch (6 mm) of oil in a large skillet over medium heat until it begins to shimmer. Working with four to six pieces at a time, carefully add the toasts to the pan, coconut side down, and pan-fry until the coconut is golden brown and the shrimp is cooked through, about 2 minutes. They may splatter, so use caution. Flip over the toasts and cook the other side until browned, 1 minute longer, adjusting the heat as necessary so the toasts don't burn. Transfer the toasts to a paper towel–lined tray to drain and then serve immediately with the sweet and sour strawberry sauce on the side.

PARTY PEOPLE PEPPERONI PIZZA POCKETS (PPPPP)

serves 8 as a party snack

This recipe is what you get when you cross Totino's Pizza Rolls with Bagel Bites. In other words, your childhood is calling. It wants you to ask your mom if you can come over for dinner and maybe even spend the night. Our version uses a basic pepperoni and cheese filling, but by all means, get creative. Add sausage, onions, mushrooms, peppers, pineapple, Canadian bacon, or whatever you want. The only requirement is that you have to cook it first. Raw vegetables will release water and make the pockets soggy, and raw meat may not cook all the way through in time. Simply throw whatever addition you want into a skillet, add a splash of oil, and cook over medium-high heat for a few minutes, until the water cooks off or the meat is cooked through. The best thing about this recipe is that you can keep these stocked in your freezer at all times and pop them in the oven whenever you or your inner child gets a late-night snack attack.

2 cups (280 g) all-purpose flour, plus more for dusting

2 teaspoons baking powder

½ teaspoon kosher salt, plus more for seasoning

¼ teaspoon baking soda

⅔ cup (147 g) Greek yogurt

⅔ cup (160 ml) heavy cream

One 14-ounce (397 g) can crushed tomatoes

2 tablespoons olive oil

1 garlic clove, smashed

4 ounces (113 g) low-moisture mozzarella, finely diced or shredded (about 1 cup)

3 ounces (85 g) pepperoni, finely diced

Olive oil, for brushing

FREEZABLE

SPECIAL EQUIPMENT
Blender

HACKABLE
Use store-bought tomato sauce.

PREP AHEAD
PPPPP can be made up to a month in advance and stored in the freezer. Bake from frozen. The sauce can be made up to 5 days in advance and stored in the fridge.

1 Whisk together the flour, baking powder, salt, and baking soda in a medium bowl. Add the yogurt and heavy cream, and stir until a dough forms. If the dough feels dry, add a little water, 1 tablespoon at a time. Knead the dough for just a minute to help it hydrate evenly.

2 Place the dough on a lightly floured work surface, and divide it into 32 equal portions. Roll the portions into balls slightly smaller than a golf or ping-pong ball. Cover the balls with a layer of plastic wrap, and let them rest for 30 minutes.

3 While the dough rests, add the tomatoes, olive oil, and garlic to a blender and blend until smooth. Season with salt.

4 Mix ⅔ cup (160 ml) of the tomato sauce with the mozzarella and pepperoni in a small bowl. Add the rest of the tomato sauce to a small pot, and set aside.

5 Line a baking sheet with parchment paper, and dust a work surface lightly with flour. Working in batches of eight, press the dough balls into 3-inch (7.5 cm) rounds. Add 1 heaping teaspoon of filling to the center of a round, pull up the sides, and pinch the dough around the filling to fully enclose it. Flip over the pocket so the seam is on the bottom, and place it on the prepared baking sheet. Repeat with the remaining dough balls and filling, making sure the pockets don't touch when you add them to the baking sheet. (It's okay if they are close together.) Use scissors or a paring knife to score a small X on the top of each pocket and place them in the freezer for at least 1 hour, up to 1 month.

6 Preheat the oven to 400°F (200°C). Line another baking sheet with parchment paper.

7 Working in batches, arrange the pockets at least 2 inches (5 cm) apart on the baking sheet. Brush each pocket with olive oil. Bake for 20 to 25 minutes, until golden brown. Repeat as necessary with the remaining pockets.

8 While the pockets bake, bring the remaining tomato sauce to a simmer over medium heat. Reduce the heat to medium-low, and simmer for about 5 minutes to allow the flavors to meld.

9 Serve the pockets with the warmed sauce on the side for dipping.

BEEFY ITALIAN SLIDERS

makes 24 sliders

This is not, we repeat, *not* an authentic Italian beef recipe. This is our *ode* to the Italian beef, so please don't come for us re: authenticity. We love this recipe for parties because a) it's freaking delicious, and b) it's easy to assemble and feed a crowd. We tested both sweet Hawaiian rolls and savory potato rolls. Half of us liked the sweet ones best, and the other half preferred the potato. We leave the decision on which to use up to you. Serve these with some Chow Chow (page 31) or a pile of pickles on the side.

2 pounds (907 g) boneless beef short ribs or brisket

Kosher salt and freshly ground black pepper

2 tablespoons grapeseed or canola oil

1 yellow onion, roughly chopped

6 garlic cloves, thinly sliced

4 cups (960 ml) reduced-sodium beef broth

2 teaspoons garlic powder

2 teaspoons onion powder

2 teaspoons dried oregano

2 teaspoons dried thyme

1 teaspoon browning and seasoning sauce (Kitchen Bouquet preferred)

1 teaspoon celery seeds

1 teaspoon red pepper flakes

1 teaspoon sweet or hot paprika

Two packages 12-piece slider rolls or sweet Hawaiian rolls

2 cups (256 g) drained Giardiniera (page 32), chopped, or one 16-ounce (480 ml) jar giardiniera, drained and roughly chopped

8 ounces (227 g) sliced provolone

1 cup (220 g) Pepperoncini Aioli (page 40)

1 Preheat the oven to 325°F (165°C).

2 Season the short ribs liberally with salt and pepper. Heat the oil in a large Dutch oven over medium-high heat. Add the ribs, and sear on all sides until browned, 2 to 3 minutes per side. Remove the beef from the pot and set aside.

3 Add the onion and cook until it starts to brown, about 1 minute. Add the garlic and cook for an additional 30 seconds. Add the beef broth, and scrape the bottom of the pan with a wooden spoon to get any bits off the bottom. Add the garlic powder, onion powder, oregano, thyme, browning and seasoning sauce, celery seeds, red pepper flakes, and paprika. Season with more salt and pepper, and bring to a simmer. Return the beef and all of its juices back to the pot, and flip it around in the liquid to give it a bath.

4 Bring the mixture to a simmer, cover, and place in the oven for 3 to 4 hours, until the beef is very soft and falling apart. Remove from the oven, and use two forks to shred the beef into chunks right there in its juices. Let the beef cool to room temperature in said juices. Taste and season with more salt if needed.

5 When you are ready to make the sliders, heat the oven to 350°F (180°C) and line a 9 × 13-inch (23 × 33 cm) pan with foil, leaving a 2-inch (5 cm) overhang of foil on opposite sides of the pan. (These will act as lifters later.)

6 Strain the beef from its juices, if needed. (You want the beef to be moist, but if it's too juicy, it will sog out the slider rolls.) You should have about 4 cups (800 g) of the shredded beef filling.

7 Remove the slider rolls from their packages and slice each package as a whole unit, horizontally right down the middle, creating two top "sheets" and two bottom "sheets." Arrange the bottom sheets in the prepared pan. (You might need to squeeze them a little to get them to fit.) Spoon the beef on top, top with the giardiniera, and cover it all with the provolone. Spread the Pepperoncini Aioli on the cut sides of the top sheets and place the sheets onto the cheese, cut-side down, to make sandwiches.

8 Cover the pan with foil and bake for about 30 minutes, until the cheese has melted and the bread is a little browned and toasty. Remove the foil for the last 10 minutes of cooking to toast the tops of the rolls.

9 Remove from the oven, and let cool for 5 minutes. Use the foil lifters to transfer the sliders out of the pan and onto a platter. Pull apart the individual sandwiches, and eat while hot.

FREEZABLE

PREP AHEAD
The beef can be made up to 3 days in advance and stored in the fridge, or it can be frozen for up to 1 month. Thaw and reheat it before assembling the sandwiches.

HACKABLE
Use store-bought giardiniera and 4 cups (480 g) thinly sliced store-bought roast beef. Heat 1 cup (240 ml) of the beef broth with half the spices, and soak the roast beef in it for a few minutes before adding it to the rolls in step 7.

sweets

Although not fully necessary, it's always nice to offer dessert. Those who have a sweet tooth will love you forever, and those who don't will probably at least appreciate the gesture. This chapter is divided into two sections: *sheet cakes* and *not sheet cakes.* As you've probably guessed, the sheet cakes section is chock-full of sheet cakes. We went in this direction because, as a professional cake-maker and a semiprofessional cake-eater, respectively, Courtney and Brie know how daunting cake assembly can be, especially for those who don't do it regularly. There's no need to waste time assembling a fancy layer cake when you can wow everyone with a single-layer stunner instead. These are easy to make and easy to eat, making them the best of both worlds. As for the not sheet cakes section, these are all the recipes that didn't fit into the "sheet cake" category. It's as simple as that!

PINEAPPLE RIGHT-SIDE-UP CAKE

serves 8 to 12

Pineapple upside-down cake gets to have all the fun, and we say *no more!* Here, we put the pineapples inside the cake, instead of underneath it. We also add some to the frosting, along with boxed yellow cake mix for that vintage Betty Crocker feeling (even though we prefer the Duncan Hines flavor profile best). The Food and Drug Administration strongly advises against eating raw flour, so we heat-treat the cake mix before using it. Top the finished cake with a handful of maraschino cherries to make it extra cute.

PINEAPPLES

1 medium pineapple, cored and cut into ½-inch (1 cm) chunks (about 6 cups/907 g)

¼ cup (60 g) light brown sugar, firmly packed

¼ teaspoon kosher salt

2 tablespoons unsalted butter, cut into small chunks

CAKE BATTER

Butter or pan spray, for greasing

1½ sticks (12 tablespoons) unsalted butter, softened

1½ cups (300 g) granulated sugar

⅓ cup (75 g) light brown sugar, firmly packed

3 eggs

3 egg yolks

1½ tablespoons vanilla extract

½ cup (120 ml) grapeseed or canola oil

2¼ cups (338 g) cake flour

1½ teaspoons baking powder

1¼ teaspoons kosher salt

¾ teaspoon baking soda

1 cup (240 ml) buttermilk

YELLOW CAKE FROSTING

1 cup (160 g) boxed yellow cake mix

2 sticks (16 tablespoons) unsalted butter, softened

1 cup (125 g) confectioners' sugar

1 tablespoon half-and-half

1 teaspoon vanilla extract

Maraschino cherries in their liquid

1 Preheat the oven to 450°F (230°C). Line a baking sheet with parchment paper.

2 Make the pineapples: Spread the pineapple chunks on the baking sheet. Toss with the brown sugar and salt and then dot with the butter. Bake for 45 to 55 minutes, tossing halfway through, until the pineapples are very soft and caramelized and most of the liquid has evaporated from the pan. Remove from the oven, and use a spatula to scrape the pineapples and all the butter and sugary juices into a bowl or container. Chill in the fridge for at least 1 hour and up to 4 days.

3 Reduce the oven temperature to 350°F (180°C). Grease a 9 × 13-inch (23 × 33 cm) baking pan with butter or pan spray, and line the bottom with parchment paper.

4 Make the cake batter: Add the butter, granulated sugar, and brown sugar to the bowl of a stand mixer fitted with the paddle attachment. Start the mixer on low (so you don't spray sugar everywhere) and then work your way up to high,

and cream until light, fluffy, and emulsified, about 4 minutes, stopping to scrape down the sides of the bowl a couple times.

5 Meanwhile, crack the eggs into a liquid measuring cup (it's easier to add them this way), add the egg yolks, and measure the vanilla on top of the eggs.

6 Reduce the mixer speed to medium, and add the eggs, one or two at a time, waiting 10 to 15 seconds between additions and scraping down the sides of the bowl several times. Increase the speed to high and mix for about 30 seconds while you measure the oil into the liquid measuring cup. Reduce the speed to medium-low, and slowly drizzle in the oil. Ramp it back up to high, and let 'er rip for a minute or two, until the mixture is very light and fluffy and gorgeous.

7 Meanwhile, whisk together the flour, baking powder, salt, and baking soda in a large bowl.

8 Measure the buttermilk into the now-empty liquid measuring cup. (See how we are saving you from creating a bunch of dirty dishes?)

9   Scrape down the sides of the mixer bowl, and with the mixer on low, add one-third of the flour mixture to the batter, then half of the buttermilk, then half of the remaining flour, then the rest of the buttermilk, and finally the last of the flour. Increase the mixer speed to medium, and mix for about 30 seconds to make sure the batter is evenly combined. Scrape the bowl one last time, all the way down to the bottom, and if you notice any streaks, do any extra mixing by hand.

10 Measure out 1½ cups (240 g) of the roasted pineapple, finely chop it, add it to the batter, and mix on low until evenly combined.

11 Pour the batter into the prepared pan, and use a spoon or spatula to make sure it's evenly distributed. Bake for about 40 minutes, rotating after 30 minutes, until the cake starts to brown on the edges, bounces back slightly when you press on the top, and just starts to pull away from the sides.

12 Remove from the oven, and let cool to room temperature. Transfer to the fridge to chill for 2 hours.

13 Preheat the oven to 325°F (165°C).

14 Make the frosting: Evenly spread the yellow cake mix onto a baking sheet. Bake for 10 minutes, until it reaches a temperature of 160°F (71°C). Remove from the oven and cool completely before adding to the frosting in step 17.

15 Meanwhile, measure out 1 cup (160 g) of the roasted pineapple, finely chop it, and set it aside. Reserve any leftover pineapple to decorate the top of the cake or to snack on.

16 Add the butter to the bowl of a stand mixer fitted with the paddle attachment, and let 'er rip on high until the butter is whipped and completely smooth, about 2 minutes, stopping to scrape down the sides of the bowl a couple times.

17 Add the confectioners' sugar and cake mix. Start the mixer on low (to prevent a sugar explosion) and then gradually work up to high. Whip on high speed until the frosting is the lightest and fluffiest, about 2 minutes. Add the chopped pineapples, half-and-half, and vanilla, and mix on low to combine.

18 To decorate the cake, remove it from the fridge, invert it onto a large platter, and remove the parchment paper. Alternately, just keep it in the pan. Use a pastry brush or spoon to soak the top of the cake with about 3 tablespoons of the liquid from the maraschino cherry jar.

19 Spread the frosting over the top of the soaked cake. Make it flat, or do swoops and swirls, whatever you feel. Decorate the top of the cake with maraschino cherries, cut, and serve.

FREEZABLE

SPECIAL EQUIPMENT
Stand mixer with paddle attachment or hand mixer

NOTE
If you don't have a stand mixer, you can use an old-school hand mixer, or you could mix all of this by hand, but you'll need some massive elbow grease to do so.

PREP AHEAD
Make the pineapples up to 4 days in advance. Make the frosting up to 1 week in advance. Bring to room temperature and mix to loosen before decorating. The baked cake, either by itself or fully assembled, can be stored in the fridge for up to 3 days or frozen for up to 1 month. Bring to room temperature before serving.

COURTNEY'S GRANDMA'S TEXAS SHEET CAKE

serves 8 to 12

Throughout her childhood, Courtney would feast on this chocolate fudge and pecan-topped cake every time she went to her grandma's house. (This is the same grandma who gifted her *The Care Bears' Party Cookbook*, by the way.) That's pretty normal for a Texan, as this is a classic mid-century recipe that graces Lone Star tables often. These cakes are traditionally made in a jelly roll pan, which is 15 × 10 inches (38 × 25 cm). Although the jelly roll pan is ideal, you could bake this in a 9 × 13-inch (23 × 33 cm) baking pan instead; the cake will just be a bit taller. Be sure to use natural cocoa powder, not Dutch processed; we need its acidity to interact with the baking soda and help the cake rise. It's integral to ice the cake while it's hot so the icing soaks into it, creating an extra-moist and fudgy crumb. The roasted pecans on top are a classic, but optional, touch. Courtney's grandma would only put pecans on half of her cake so the people who didn't like nuts (ahem . . . *Courtney's dad*) would have options. As an added treat, there's no stand mixer required to make this. It's all done by hand.

CAKE

Butter or pan spray, for greasing

¼ cup (25 g) unsweetened natural cocoa powder

2 sticks (16 tablespoons) unsalted butter

2 cups (280 g) all-purpose flour

2 cups (400 g) granulated sugar

1 teaspoon baking soda

¾ teaspoon kosher salt

½ cup (120 ml) buttermilk

2 eggs, beaten

1 teaspoon vanilla extract

FROSTING

3½ cups (437 g) confectioners' sugar

3 tablespoons unsweetened natural cocoa powder

¼ teaspoon kosher salt

1 stick (8 tablespoons) unsalted butter, melted

⅓ cup (80 ml) whole milk

1 cup (112 g) toasted pecan pieces (optional)

FREEZABLE

PREP AHEAD
The finished cake can be stored in fridge for up to 4 days or frozen for up to 1 month. Bring to room temperature before serving.

1 Preheat the oven to 350°F (180°C). Grease a 15 × 10-inch (38 × 25 cm) jelly roll pan with butter or pan spray, and line the bottom with parchment paper.

2 Make the cake: Whisk together the cocoa powder and 1 cup (240 ml) water in a small pot. Set over medium-high heat, add the butter, and bring the mixture to a boil. The butter should be melted by the time it boils; if not, reduce the heat to low and continue heating until the butter melts. Remove from the heat, and let cool for 5 minutes.

3 Whisk together the flour, granulated sugar, baking soda, and salt in a large bowl.

4 Whisk the buttermilk into the cocoa-and-butter mixture and then add the eggs and vanilla. Pour the liquid mixture into the dry mixture, and whisk until smooth.

5 Pour the batter into the cake pan, and bake for about 40 minutes, until the cake bounces back slightly when you press on the top and just starts to pull away from the sides.

6 While the cake bakes, prepare the frosting: Mix together the confectioners' sugar, cocoa powder, and salt in another large bowl. Add the melted butter and milk, and mix to combine. It's okay if there are a few small clumps of confectioners' sugar; they will dissolve when you ice the cake. Stir in the pecans, if using.

7 Remove the cake from the oven, and let it cool for 5 minutes. While it's still hot, spread the frosting over the top. It will spread easily as the heat melts it.

8 Cool the cake to room temperature before slicing and serving. The frosting will set as it cools.

AMORE AMARO CAKE

serves 8 to 12

This incredibly moist cake harnesses the power of amaro, olive oil, and a little bit of orange for a lovely floral and fruity flavor. For best results, use a less-bitter amaro, like Nardini or CioCiaro, and make sure your olive oil is quality. It doesn't need to be expensive, but it should taste good, because you'll be able to taste it in the finished product. We top the cake with barely sweetened whipped cream and crushed raspberries. You'll probably have a little extra, so serve what's left on the side for people to spoon on top of their slices. As an added treat, there's no stand mixer required to make this. It's all done by hand.

CAKE

2 cups (280 g) all-purpose flour

1½ cups (300 g) granulated sugar

1¼ teaspoons kosher salt

½ teaspoon baking powder

½ teaspoon baking soda

1½ cups (360 ml) olive oil, plus more for greasing

1½ cups (360 ml) whole milk

¼ cup (60 ml) Italian amaro, like Amaro Nardini

¼ cup (60 ml) fresh orange juice (from 1 large orange)

2 eggs

2 egg yolks

1½ teaspoons finely grated orange zest (from that same large orange)

WHIPPED TOPPING

12 ounces (340 g) fresh raspberries

2 tablespoons granulated sugar

1½ cups (360 ml) heavy cream

½ cup (62 g) confectioners' sugar

½ cup (110 g) Lime Crème Fraîche (page 41)

1 Preheat the oven to 350°F (180°C). Grease a 9 × 13-inch (23 × 33 cm) cake pan with olive oil, and line the bottom with parchment paper.

2 Make the cake: Whisk together the flour, granulated sugar, salt, baking powder, and baking soda in a large bowl.

3 Whisk together the olive oil, milk, amaro, orange juice, eggs, egg yolks, and orange zest in a separate large bowl. Pour the olive oil mixture into the flour mixture, and mix until just combined.

4 Pour the batter into the cake pan, and bake for about 35 minutes, until the cake starts to brown on the edges, bounces back slightly when you press on the top, and just starts to pull away from the sides. Remove from the oven, and cool to room temperature. Transfer to the fridge to chill for 2 hours.

5 To finish the cake, remove it from the fridge, invert it onto a platter, and remove the parchment paper from the bottom, or just keep it in the pan.

6 Make the whipped topping: Toss the raspberries and granulated sugar in a medium bowl. Use the back of a fork to crush the raspberries so they release some of their juices. Don't pulverize them; just lightly crush them. Set aside.

7 Add the heavy cream and confectioners' sugar to a large bowl, and whisk to medium-soft peaks. Add the crème fraîche and continue whipping to medium-firm peaks. (You can use a mixer on medium-high for this if you prefer.)

8 Spread the whipped cream mixture over the top of the cake. Drain the crushed raspberries from their juices and top the cake with a spoonful of them. Slice and serve with the leftover raspberries on the side.

FREEZABLE

PREP AHEAD
The baked cake, by itself, can be stored in the fridge for up to 3 days or frozen for up to 1 month. Once frosted, it's best eaten the same day. Bring to room temperature before serving.

HACKABLE
Sub store-bought crème fraîche or sour cream for the Lime Crème Fraîche.

CANDY CHERRY RITZ CAKE

serves 8 to 12

Ritz crackers are America's croissant. There, we said it. We all grew up eating them, and just like we do with other tasty foods from childhood, once we become "adults," we brush them under the rug and pretend we are too fancy to enjoy them. But to us, the true mark of maturation, intelligence, and "adulthood" is to boldly put a stack of Ritz on a charcuterie or cheese board. Try it, and watch what happens. People will wonder if it's allowed. They'll give you the side-eye. But eventually they'll gobble them up with huge smiles on their crumb-covered faces. That's the power of Ritz. We use them two ways in this cake: as a crunchy topping and ground up as a partial flour substitute. This "Ritz flour" gives the batter less structure, and she falls more easily, so don't jiggle the cake or check it too early or often as it bakes. Just let it do its thing, and you will be handsomely rewarded in the end. As for the frosting, if you don't like cherry, use any flavor of unsweetened Kool-Aid powder you like. Grape would be an excellent choice. Any leftover frosting can be slathered onto more Ritz crackers and put out on a charcuterie or cheese board.

RITZ CRUNCH

30 butter crackers, like Ritz (from about 1 sleeve)

¼ cup (50 g) granulated sugar

¼ teaspoon kosher salt

1 stick (8 tablespoons) unsalted butter, melted

RITZ CAKE BATTER

45 butter crackers, like Ritz (from about 1½ sleeves)

Butter or pan spray, for greasing

1½ sticks (12 tablespoons) unsalted butter, softened

1½ cups (300 g) granulated sugar

½ cup (112 g) light brown sugar, firmly packed

3 eggs

3 egg yolks

1 tablespoon vanilla extract

¾ cup (180 ml) grapeseed or canola oil

2 cups (300 g) cake flour

1½ teaspoons baking powder

1¼ teaspoons kosher salt

¾ teaspoon baking soda

1½ cups (360 ml) buttermilk

CANDY CHERRY FROSTING

6 ounces (170 g) cream cheese, softened

3 sticks (24 tablespoons) unsalted butter, softened

⅛ teaspoon kosher salt

3 cups (375 g) confectioners' sugar

1 tablespoon half-and-half or heavy cream, plus 3 tablespoons for soaking

1 teaspoon vanilla extract

One 0.13-ounce (3.6 g) package unsweetened cherry Kool-Aid powder

1 Preheat the oven to 325°F (165°C). Line a large, rimmed baking sheet with parchment paper.

2 Make the Ritz crunch: Add the crackers, granulated sugar, and salt to a large bowl. Use your hands to toss the ingredients together, crushing the crackers into coarse crumbs and chunks (nothing larger than a penny). Add the melted butter, and toss until the crackers are evenly coated and have soaked up the butter and clump together.

3 Spread the mixture in a single layer onto the prepared baking sheet, and bake for about 20 minutes, tossing halfway through, until the crumbs are toasty and browned on the top and edges. Remove from the oven, and cool to room temperature.

4 Make the cake batter: Put the butter crackers in a large zipper-top bag, and use a rolling pin or a mallet to crush them into fine crumbs. You should

have about 1½ cups (135 g) of crumbs. Add or remove crumbs to achieve this exact measurement, and set them aside.

5 Increase the oven temperature to 350°F (180°C). Grease a 9 × 13-inch (23 × 33 cm) baking pan with butter or pan spray, and line the bottom with parchment paper.

6 Add the butter, granulated sugar, and brown sugar to the bowl of a stand mixer fitted with the paddle attachment (see Note). Starting on low and working your way up to high (so as not to spray sugar everywhere), cream the butter and sugars until light and fluffy and emulsified, about 4 minutes, stopping to scrape down the sides of the bowl a couple times.

7 Meanwhile, crack the eggs into a liquid measuring cup (it's easier to add them this way), add the egg yolks, and measure the vanilla on top of the eggs.

8 Reduce the mixer to medium, and add the eggs, one or two at a time, waiting 10 to 15 seconds between additions and scraping down the sides of the bowl halfway through. Scrape down the sides of the bowl once again, and mix on high while you measure the oil into the liquid measuring cup. Reduce the speed to medium-low, and slowly drizzle in the oil. Ramp it back up to high, and let 'er rip to fully incorporate the oil, about 1 minute. Be careful not to over-aerate the batter, lest your cake fall in the oven. Remember, we are subbing quite a bit of the flour for ground butter crackers, so this cake can get a little testy if not handled right.

9 Meanwhile, whisk together the flour, baking powder, salt, and baking soda in a medium bowl. Stir in the 1½ cups (135 g) of cracker crumbs.

10 Measure the buttermilk in the liquid measuring cup.

11 Scrape down the sides of the mixer bowl again and, with the mixer on low, add one-third of the flour mixture, then half of the buttermilk, then half of the remaining flour, then the rest of the buttermilk, followed by the last of the flour. Turn the mixer up to medium, and mix to make sure the batter is evenly combined, about 15 seconds. Scrape the bowl one last time, all the way down to the bottom, and if you notice any streaks, do the extra mixing by hand.

12 Pour the batter into the prepared pan, and use a spoon or spatula to make sure it's evenly distributed. Bake for about 35 minutes, until the cake starts to brown on the edges, bounces back slightly when you press on the top, and just starts to pull away from the sides. Remove from the oven, and let cool to room temperature. Chill in the fridge for 2 hours.

13 Make the frosting and assemble the cake: Add the cream cheese, butter, and salt to the bowl of the stand mixer fitted with the paddle attachment, and let 'er rip on high until the mixture is whipped and completely smooth, about 2 minutes, stopping to scrape down the sides of the bowl a couple times along the way.

14 Add the confectioners' sugar. Start the mixer on low and then gradually work up to high, thus preventing a sugar explosion. Continue to mix on high until the frosting is the lightest and fluffiest, about 2 minutes, scraping down the sides of the bowl as needed.

15 Turn the mixer to low. Add the 1 tablespoon half-and-half, the vanilla, and the Kool-Aid powder, and mix to combine.

16 To decorate the cake, remove it from the fridge, invert it onto a platter, and remove the parchment paper from the bottom, or just keep it in the pan. Use a pastry brush or a spoon to soak the top of the cake with the remaining 3 tablespoons half-and-half.

17 Spread 1½ cups (300 g) frosting over the top of the cake to act as glue and then sprinkle 1 cup (60 g) Ritz crunch on top of the frosting. Top with another 2 to 3½ cups of frosting, depending on how much you love frosting, and spread it out over the Ritz crunch. You can spread it flat, make swoops and swirls, or style it however you want.

18 Decorate the top of the cake with the rest of the Ritz crunch and then place it in the fridge for at least an hour. Bring to room temperature before cutting and serving.

FREEZABLE

SPECIAL EQUIPMENT
Rolling pin, stand mixer with paddle attachment or hand mixer

NOTE
If you don't have a stand mixer, you can use an old-school hand mixer, or you could mix all of this by hand, but you'll need some massive elbow grease to do so.

HACKABLE
Whip the Kool-Aid powder into two 16-ounce (454 g) tubs of store-bought cream cheese frosting instead of making the frosting from scratch.

PREP AHEAD
The Ritz crunch can be made up to 1 month in advance, and the frosting can be made up to 1 week in advance. Store each in airtight containers in the fridge. The baked cake, by itself or fully assembled, can be stored in the fridge for up to 3 days or frozen for up to 1 month. Bring to room temperature before serving.

BROWN BUTTER PECAN BLONDIES

serves 8

Both Brie and Courtney spent many youthful nights in the nineties at Applebee's, scooched up to the table, gorging on maple butter blondies. They were served in a sizzling skillet, topped with ice cream, and covered in maple butter sauce, all for only $4.99. "Blondies really do have more fun!" is what the menu said, and it's true, they do. Our version uses brown butter for an even nuttier flavor. The finished batter is quite thick—more like a soft cookie dough—so you'll press it into the pan, not pour it like a typical brownie batter. Serve this warm with ice cream and a drizzle of maple syrup for the full Applebee's effect.

2 sticks (16 tablespoons) unsalted butter

2 cups (280 g) all-purpose flour

½ teaspoon baking powder

½ teaspoon kosher salt

¼ teaspoon baking soda

1¾ cups (394 g) light brown sugar, firmly packed

2 eggs

1 tablespoon vanilla extract

¾ cup (90 g) toasted pecan pieces

½ cup (85 g) white or milk chocolate or butterscotch pieces (optional)

1 Preheat the oven to 350°F (180°C). Line an 8-inch (20 cm) square baking dish with parchment paper, leaving a 2-inch (5 cm) overhang on opposite sides.

2 Melt the butter in a large pot over medium-high heat and continue to cook, swirling the pan around often, until the foam turns brown and smells nutty, about 3 minutes. Watch it carefully after the 2-minute mark, because butter can go from browned to burned quite quickly. Remove from the heat, and let cool until it's almost room temperature, but not set, about 20 minutes. It will continue to darken as it cools.

3 Whisk together the flour, baking powder, salt, and baking soda in a large bowl. Set aside.

4 Add the cooled brown butter and brown sugar to a separate large bowl, and whisk to combine. It will look like wet sand. Add the eggs and vanilla, and whisk vigorously until smooth and slightly lighter in color.

5 Use a firm spatula or wooden spoon to fold the flour mixture into the sugar mixture until just combined. The batter will be quite thick. Stir in the pecan pieces and the chocolate or butterscotch pieces (if using).

6 Press the batter evenly into the prepared baking dish, and bake for 30 to 40 minutes, until the sides just start to brown and a toothpick comes out almost clean, but with a few crumbs still on it.

7 Let the blondies cool fully before using the parchment to lift them out of the pan and slicing into squares.

NOTE

It helps to make the brown butter in a light-colored pot so you can see the color change.

PREP AHEAD

Make the brown butter up to 3 months in advance. Store in an airtight container in the fridge and soften before using.

COCONUT CRISPY TREAT BLOB

serves 8 to 12

The secret to the best Rice Krispie treats is not to press on them and condense them as they cool. That's why we are simply going to pour them onto a large sheet of parchment paper and let them take whatever shape they want. If you time it right, your guests can pull them apart and eat them while they're still warm, or if they've cooled and set up, use a knife to cut nuggets. Freshly purchased marshmallows melt better, so don't use an old bag that's been in your pantry for a thousand years.

Nonstick spray or butter, for greasing

1¾ sticks (14 tablespoons) unsalted butter

2½ cups (150 g) unsweetened coconut shreds

Two 16-ounce (454 g) bags marshmallows

8 cups (200 g) puffed rice cereal

¾ teaspoon kosher salt

1 Line a baking sheet or a heat-proof baking sheet–sized serving tray with parchment paper, and lightly grease it with nonstick spray or butter.

2 Melt the butter in a large pot over medium-high heat. Stir in the coconut, and cook until the coconut begins to brown on the edges, about 3 minutes.

3 Reduce the heat to low, add the marshmallows, and stir until they are completely melted. Add the rice cereal and salt and stir until combined.

4 Pour the mixture onto the parchment paper.

5 Serve immediately while warm for epic marshmallow pulls, or let it cool to room temperature and tell everyone to break themselves off a lil' treat.

PARTY PEOPLE POP-TART PEACH PIE (PPP-TPP)

serves 8 to 10

Here, a thin layer of peach filling is sandwiched between crumbly shortbread crusts, giving us something akin to if a Pop-Tart and a peach pie had a baby. You can use frozen peaches if fresh aren't available. Be sure to thaw them first before going on with step 9. Courtney made this for Hot Dog Appreciation Club Festival '24, and everyone raved about it.

DOUGH

3 sticks (24 tablespoons) unsalted butter, softened

1 cup (125 g) confectioners' sugar

¾ teaspoon kosher salt

3 cups (420 g) all-purpose flour

Butter or pan spray, for greasing

1 egg, beaten with 1 teaspoon water

FILLING

2 pounds (907 g) ripe peaches, peeled and pitted

1 cup (200 g) granulated sugar

⅓ cup (46 g) all-purpose flour

1 tablespoon lemon juice

Kosher salt

PREP AHEAD

The pie dough can be made and chilled up to 4 days in advance. The pie can be baked 1 day in advance, but it's best eaten on the same day it's baked. The raw pie can be assembled through step 10 and frozen for up to 1 month. Bake from frozen, according to steps 8 and 11, adding on a few minutes of bake time, if needed.

SPECIAL EQUIPMENT

Stand mixer with paddle attachment or hand mixer

NOTE

If you don't have a stand mixer, you can use an old-school hand mixer, or you could mix all of this by hand, but you'll need some massive elbow grease to do so.

HACKABLE

Frozen peaches or other fruits can be used. Thaw before using.

1 Make the dough: Add the butter to the bowl of a stand mixer fitted with the paddle attachment (see Note), and cream on high until light and fluffy, about 2 minutes. Scrape down the sides of the bowl.

2 Add the confectioners' sugar and salt. Starting on low and working your way up to high (so as not to spray sugar everywhere), cream until light and fluffy and emulsified, about 4 minutes, stopping to scrape down the sides of the bowl a couple times.

3 Add the flour in one addition, and mix on low until it's just combined and a dough forms.

4 Line a 9 × 13-inch (23 × 33 cm) pan with parchment paper with a 2-inch (5 cm) overhang on opposite sides. (These are lifters; you'll use them later, we promise.) Don't grease the pan.

5 Divide the dough in half. Each half should be about 7 ounces (198 g). Use your hands to press half of the dough into the pan in an even layer about ¼-inch-thick (6 mm). Use a fork to prick the dough all over. Use the lifters to remove the dough and place it in the freezer.

6 Grease the pan with butter or pan spray, and line it with another piece of parchment paper with a 2-inch (5 cm) overhang on opposite sides.

7 Use your hand to press the other half of the dough into the pan in an even layer and then prick it all over with a fork. Keep the dough in the pan this time, and place it in the freezer, too. Both doughs need to chill for 15 minutes, which is great because you have work to do.

8 Preheat the oven to 400°F (200°C).

9 Make the filling: Add the peaches to a medium bowl, and crush them by hand into small chunks no larger than a hazelnut. (If you can't crush them, that means they probably aren't ripe enough. Try again later.) Stir in the granulated sugar, flour, and lemon juice, and add a pinch of salt for good measure. You should have about 3½ cups (900 g) of peach filling. It will seem waaaay too liquidy, but that's what you want.

10 Remove the dough in the pan from the freezer, and pour the filling evenly over the top. Place the second layer of dough on top of the filling, and press down gently. Brush the top with egg wash.

11 Place the pie in the oven, and immediately reduce the oven temperature to 350°F (180°C). Bake for 40 to 50 minutes, until the top is golden brown and the filling is bubbling. Re-poke the fork holes halfway through baking if needed. Remove from the oven, and allow to cool to room temperature. Chill in the fridge for a least an hour.

12 Use the lifters to remove the chilled pie from the pan, slice, and serve. The pie tastes great slightly chilled or at room temperature.

SALTED MARGARITA PIE

serves 6 to 8

Here we took a perfectly respectable but extremely stressed-out key lime pie and loosened it up with some tequila. It ate the worm, and now its necktie is around its forehead, the top five buttons of its shirt are completely undone, and it's on the dance floor doing the macarena with someone 20 years its junior. It looks absolutely ridiculous, but hey, we all need to have a little fun sometimes. Purchase pre-crumbed graham crackers or put whole ones in a zipper-top bag and use a rolling pin or mallet to smash them. You can throw this pie back on the wagon and omit the booze altogether, if desired. Like we said, it's a perfectly respectable key lime pie recipe otherwise.

CRUST

1½ cups (4.5 ounces/127 g) graham cracker crumbs

½ cup (2 ounces/57 g) finely crushed tortilla chips

3 tablespoons granulated sugar

¼ teaspoon kosher salt

1¼ sticks (10 tablespoons) unsalted butter, melted

FILLING

One 14-ounce (397 g) can sweetened condensed milk

4 egg yolks

⅓ cup (80 ml) fresh lime juice

2 tablespoons tequila blanco

1 teaspoon lime zest

TOPPING

1 teaspoon Chile Lime Salt (page 36)

2 teaspoons lime zest

1 cup (240 ml) heavy cream

⅓ cup (42 g) confectioners' sugar

¼ cup (55 g) sour cream

1 tablespoon Cointreau

1 Preheat the oven to 375°F (190°C).

2 Make the crust: Add the graham cracker and tortilla chip crumbs to a large bowl, and stir in the granulated sugar and salt. Add the butter, and mix to combine.

3 Press the mixture into a 9-inch (23 cm) pie pan, and bake for 8 to 10 minutes, until the edges just start to brown. Remove from the oven, and reduce the oven temperature to 325°F (165°C).

4 Make the filling: Add the sweetened condensed milk and egg yolks to a medium bowl, and whisk until smooth. Add the lime juice, tequila, and lime zest, and pour the filling into the baked crust. Return to the oven and bake for about 15 minutes, until the filling is set but still jiggles a bit when you shake it. Remove from the oven, and allow to cool to room temperature. Chill in the fridge for at least 2 hours.

5 Make the topping: Stir together the Chile Lime Salt and lime zest in a small bowl. Set aside.

6 Add the heavy cream and confectioners' sugar to a large bowl, and whip it to medium peaks. (This can be done by hand or with a stand mixer with a whisk attachment on medium-high.) Add the sour cream and Cointreau, and continue to whip to medium-stiff peaks.

7 Spread the whipped cream mixture on top of the chilled pie, creating swoops and swirls or whatever you like. Sprinkle the top with the Chile Lime Salt mixture, slice, and serve.

SPECIAL EQUIPMENT
Stand mixer with whisk attachment or hand mixer

FREEZABLE
Make this a frozen margarita pie popsicle and eat it straight from the freezer.

PREP AHEAD
Make the pie through step 4 up to 3 days in advance. Wrap it in plastic wrap, and store in the fridge.

HACKABLE
Sub Tajín for the Chile Lime Salt.

CHEESE DANISH GALETTE

serves 8

This galette tastes remarkably like a cheese Danish, which, conveniently, is the best kind of Danish. If your puff pastry is already browned when you remove it from the oven in step 4, you can skip step 5. Different ovens brown at different rates, so use your best judgment. We swirl cherry jam on top, but any flavor would work, especially Brie's Grandma's Pomegranate Jelly (page 112). This is best served the same day it's baked.

One 10- to 14-ounce (283 to 397 g) sheet puff pastry, thawed

All-purpose flour, for dusting (optional)

1 egg, beaten

8 ounces (227 g) cream cheese, softened

⅓ cup (67 g) sugar

⅛ teaspoon kosher salt

¾ teaspoon vanilla extract

¼ cup (55 g) Lime Crème Fraîche (page 41) or sour cream

⅓ cup (112 g) good-quality cherry jam

1 Preheat the oven to 400°F (200°C). Line a baking sheet with parchment paper.

2 Working directly on the parchment paper, roll or stretch out the puff pastry to roughly a 10 × 15-inch (25 × 38 cm) rectangle. If the dough seems too sticky, lightly dust the parchment with some flour first.

3 Use a knife to score a 1-inch-thick (2.5 cm) border all around the edge of the puff pastry, being careful not to cut all the way through. Prick the bottom of the pastry with a fork (everywhere but on the border). If you want, score the border in a decorative pattern and then brush it with a tiny bit of the beaten egg. (Not too much, because you'll use the egg to make the filling later—like, use ½ teaspoon of the egg at most.)

4 Bake for 15 to 20 minutes, until the pastry is puffed and just starting to brown. Remove it from the oven, and use a mallet or flat spatula to press down on the center, inside the border, to de-puff it.

5 Return the puff pastry to the oven, and bake for 7 to 8 minutes more, until light golden brown. Remove it from the oven and press down the center again, if needed.

6 Reduce the oven temperature to 350°F (180°C).

7 Prepare the filling while the pastry bakes: Add the cream cheese to the bowl of a stand mixer fitted with the paddle attachment and beat on medium-high until smooth, about 4 minutes. Scrape down the sides of the bowl, add the sugar and salt, and cream until light and fluffy, about 4 more minutes. Scrape again, add the egg and vanilla, and mix for 1 minute. Scrape the bowl, add the Lime Crème Fraîche, and mix on low to combine.

8 Spread the filling evenly in the baked pastry shell. Dot the top with the cherry jam (if needed, loosen the jam with a little bit of water first) and then drag a toothpick or skewer through the cherry jam to make swirls.

9 Bake for 20 to 25 minutes, until the filling is set and slightly puffed. Remove from the oven, and cool for at least 1 hour before serving.

SPECIAL EQUIPMENT
Stand mixer with paddle attachment

BRIE'S GRANDMA'S POMEGRANATE JELLY
(and Three Things You Can Do with It)

makes about 5½ cups (1.7 kg)

This vibrant pink jelly tastes best when made with freshly squeezed pomegranate juice, and yes, we are aware of how annoying that is to acquire. Some farmers markets sell freshly squeezed juice, so if that's an option, go for it; otherwise, the easiest way to extract it is to gather all the seeds, throw them in a zipper-top bag, and smash them with a rolling pin. Snip off a small hole from the corner of the bag, and squeeze out the juice. This jelly is great smeared on toast or used in a PB&J, or our Cheese Danish Galette (see page 110). There are also three more things you can do with it…

3½ cups (840 ml) fresh pomegranate juice (from about 5 pomegranates)

One 1.75-ounce (49 g) package Sure-Jell fruit pectin (the yellow box)

5 cups (1 kg) sugar

1 Stir together the pomegranate juice and pectin in a large pot. Set over medium-high heat, and bring to a rolling boil. Dump all the sugar into the pot at once. (Brie's grandma says this part is very important.)

2 Bring the mixture back to a hard boil, stirring to dissolve the sugar. Continue boiling for 2 minutes and then remove from the heat.

3 Skim off any foam from the top of the jelly. Store the jelly in the fridge for up to 1 month, and keep reading for some things you can do with it.

Thing #1: Jar it up and give it away as a surprise thank-you-for-being-a-friend gift.

FREEZABLE

PREP AHEAD
Store in an airtight container in the fridge for up to 1 month or in the freezer for up to 3 months.

SPECIAL EQUIPMENT
Glass jars

While the jelly is still hot, wash and dry some glass jars with lids. The full recipe will fill five 8-ounce (240 ml) jars, with a little extra for yourself (see below, re: Cosmos). Pour the jelly in the jars, and seal each tightly. Let cool to room temperature, and keep stored in the fridge or freezer. Unless you are planning on keeping these around for months on end, or leaving them at room temperature, you don't really need to go through the whole canning process. Tie the jelly jars with a bow, and hand them out. Since these are not "properly" canned, be sure to tell your friends the proper storage instructions (see Prep Ahead).

Thing #2: Make a Pomegranate Cosmo (serves 1)

SPECIAL EQUIPMENT
Cocktail shaker, martini or coupe glass

Ice

2 ounces (60 ml) vodka

1 ounce (30 ml) Cointreau

1 ounce (30 ml) lime juice

1 tablespoon Brie's Grandma's Pomegranate Jelly

1 lime twist

1 Fill a cocktail shaker with ice. Add the vodka, Cointreau, lime juice, and Brie's Grandma's Pomegranate Jelly. Shake until cold and icy.

2 Strain into a martini or coupe glass, and garnish with a lime twist. Repeat as necessary.

Thing #3: Make Swedish pancakes (a nod to Brie's grandma, who is of Swedish descent) (serves 3 to 4)

1½ cups (360 ml) whole milk

1 cup (140 g) all-purpose flour

3 eggs

3 tablespoons unsalted butter, melted and cooled, plus more for greasing and serving

1 tablespoon granulated sugar

¼ teaspoon kosher salt

Brie's Grandma's Pomegranate Jelly (page 112)

Lemon slices

Confectioners' sugar (optional)

1 Place the milk, flour, eggs, butter, granulated sugar, and salt in a blender, and blend until smooth, about 30 seconds. Rest the batter in an airtight container in the fridge for at least 1 hour or up to overnight.

2 Grease a large nonstick skillet with butter, and set it over medium heat. Pour about 3 tablespoons of batter into the pan and then quickly tilt the pan in all directions so the batter spreads out to cover the bottom of the pan, creating thin, lacy edges.

3 Cook until the pancake is browned on the edges, about 1 minute, and then use a spatula to flip it over and cook until just set, about 10 seconds. Transfer to a plate, and repeat with the remaining batter, greasing the pan with more butter as needed, and stacking the pancakes on top of each other as they're finished. (They won't stick, but they will keep one another warm!) You should have about 10 pancakes in all.

4 Fold each pancake into quarters or roll them up into logs, and serve with big dollops of Brie's Grandma's Pomegranate Jelly, melted butter drizzled on top, lemon slices, and a generous dusting of confectioners' sugar, if you're feeling frisky.

> **PREP AHEAD**
>
> The pancake batter can be made 1 day in advance. Store in an airtight container in the fridge.

let's party

casual parties

Casual parties are just what they sound like: low stakes, easy to prep for, and super chill. Basically, they are a Late One's (page 16) dream scenario. We divided this chapter into two categories: dips and casseroles. Choose one recipe from each, add a libation, a party snack or two, and something sweet from our Party Essentials (page 45) section, and then serve it all buffet style as it's ready. For anyone wanting greens, The Simplest of Salads (page 166) in our Fancy Parties chapter would be a perfect and extremely casual addition to any menu here. Remember, if you are feeling overwhelmed, tired, strapped for cash, or just plain old lazy, you have our permission to pare this down. (Not that you need our permission, but still, you have it.) Make one of the dips, and have your friends pitch in to order takeout and some cheap beer. Again, the most important thing is to get together. Party People gotta party.

In an update that will surprise no one, we love an activity, and although you don't *have* to have one to throw a casual party, we've taken the liberty of listing a few of our favorites in the hopes that you'll adopt this mindset.

casual party activities

Book Club (read a book and talk about it)

Game Night (play board games, card games, conversation games—any game works)

Relaxing Karaoke (relax, sing, do face masks, take a nap)

Viewing Party (watch a movie, discuss the pros and cons of said movie)

PowerPoint Party (present something to the group that inspires you)

Listening Party (listen to a full album from start to finish—no skipping!)

Arts and Crafts Party (quilt, crochet, bead, color, or make anything creative—finishing the thing is optional)

Slumber Party (a super-fun add-on to any other casual party activity)

CHILE CON QUESO
(a Love Story)
serves 8 to 10

If you know Courtney McBroom, then you know of her love of queso, which is somehow even stronger than her love of hot dogs. Queso is her birthright as a Texan, and if she could marry it, she would. It also happens to be the first thing that Brie and Courtney ever connected over, which pretty much makes Brie an honorary Texan herself. Courtney has spent countless years perfecting her recipe, and you can find many versions scattered across the internet. The one printed here is approximately version 347, and it's her favorite so far.

True queso is never as simple as melting Velveeta in a slow cooker and adding a can of Ro-Tel. Although that *is* delicious, it's nothing close to Tex-Mex restaurant-style chile con queso. There's a spot in Austin called Matt's El Rancho that serves a version of queso called Bob Armstrong, named after the politician and former land commissioner of Texas. Good ol' Bob, who was a regular, waltzed into their kitchen one day and asked the owner's teenage son, Matt Martinez Jr., to give him "something different." Matt threw some taco meat, guacamole, and sour cream in the bottom of a bowl, covered it with chile con queso, and sent it out to Bob's table. At first, Bob was unimpressed, but after discovering the hidden gems nestled underneath the molten cheese, he changed his sorry tune into a love song. News of this novel queso spread quickly at the state capitol, and it's been a Texas institution ever since.

Serve your queso simply or go full-on Bob Armstrong. Hatch, poblano, or Anaheim are great picks for the green chile, and you can add a serrano if you'd like to spice it up. If you cannot find Land O'Lakes Extra Melt American cheese, Velveeta or shredded yellow American cheese will work just fine. For a quick-and-easy taco meat, make a half recipe of the Super-Fine Hot Dog Chili (page 228), omit the tomato paste and stock at the end, and add a splash of water to make it saucy. (For a real down-and-dirty version, omit the onion, jalapeño, and garlic cloves, too, since the queso already has onion, chile, and garlic powder in it.)

½ yellow onion, finely diced (about ¾ cup/100 g)

1 large green chile, seeded and finely diced (about ½ cup/55 g)

1 teaspoon powdered chicken bouillon

½ cup (120 ml) buttermilk

⅓ cup (80 ml) heavy cream

1 pound (454 g) Land O'Lakes Extra Melt American cheese, or Velveeta, cubed

2 ounces (57 g) Monterey Jack, shredded (about ½ cup)

½ teaspoon garlic powder

Tortilla chips

Pico de Gallo (page 33) or salsa

MAKE IT A BOB

Guacamole

Sour cream

Ground taco meat or black beans

1 Add the onion and green chile to a large pot, and cover with ¾ cup (180 ml) water. Set over medium-high heat, and bring to a boil. Reduce the heat to medium, and simmer until soft, about 5 minutes. Reduce the heat to low, add the bouillon, and stir to dissolve.

2 Stir in the buttermilk and heavy cream, and add the Extra Melt. Continue cooking on low, stirring often, until most of the cheese has melted, about 8 minutes.

3 Toss the Monterey Jack with the garlic powder. (This prevents the garlic powder from clumping.) Add it to the pot in three batches, stirring vigorously between additions and letting the cheese melt before adding more, until the mixture is totally smooth, about 4 minutes.

4 Taste the queso for consistency. If you want to thin it out, add up to ¼ cup (60 ml) hot water, 1 tablespoon at a time, to reach your desired

consistency. If you want it to thicken, continue cooking it over low heat, stirring often. Keep in mind that the queso will thicken significantly as it cools. Transfer it to a bowl and serve with tortilla chips and Pico de Gallo or salsa.

5 To make it a Bob, add any combination of the following: a scoop of guacamole, sour cream, taco meat, and/or black beans.

VEGETARIAN QUESO

To make this vegetarian, use vegetable bouillon instead of chicken (or omit the bouillon altogether), and black beans instead of taco meat.

PREP AHEAD

Make up to 1 week in advance. Store in an airtight container in the fridge. Before serving, reheat on the stove over low heat, in the microwave, or in a slow cooker.

FRENCH ONION RAMEN DIP

makes about 1½ cups (335 g)

It's hard to compete with the ubiquitous sour cream and onion dip, made by combining a powdered seasoning packet and tub of sour cream. Truly, it is delicious. Not as good as this, though, because we caramelize our own onions and add our favorite top-secret ingredient, Ramen Ranch Seasoning (page 43). Potato chips, corn chips, and crudité are the obvious dipping mechanisms to use, but that's just the tip of the iceberg. This goes swell with French fries, Tater Tots, pizza bites, taquitos, and potato skins, too. Don't try to rush the caramelization process, or you'll end up with subpar, burnt onions. If you find the dip to be thicker than you'd like in the end, thin it out with some buttermilk, milk, or even water. Start with 1 tablespoon and work your way up from there.

3 tablespoons unsalted butter

2 yellow onions, finely chopped (about 3 cups/400 g)

½ teaspoon sugar

Kosher salt

1 pint (454 g) sour cream

2 tablespoons Ramen Ranch Seasoning (page 43)

Juice of 1 lime

Chips or crudité, for serving

1 Heat the butter in a medium pot over medium-high heat. Add the onions, the sugar, and two good pinches of salt. The pot will be overcrowded—that's good. When the onions start sizzling hard, cover the pot and reduce the heat to medium-low. Continue to cook, stirring every 10 minutes or so, until the onions are deeply caramelized and brown, about 1 hour. If the onions begin to brown too quickly, reduce the heat further.

2 Remove from the heat, and let cool to room temperature. You should have about ½ cup (130 g) caramelized onions.

3 Stir the onions into the sour cream in a large bowl, along with the Ramen Ranch Seasoning and lime juice. Serve immediately with chips or crudité, or even better, refrigerate for 24 hours or up to 3 days.

PREP AHEAD
Make up to 3 days in advance. Store in an airtight container in the fridge.

BUFFALO CAULIFLOWER DIP

serves 6 to 8 as a party snack

Buffalo chicken on game day is a tale as old as time. Buffalo cauliflower on game day is a slightly younger tale, but a good one nonetheless. Turn either of them into a dip, and you've got a full-blown novella on your hands. We go for cauliflower here because it's vegetarian and versatile. The quickest way to make it is to grab a bag of riced cauliflower. That will yield a nice, smooth dip. For something a little chunkier, buy a medium head and cut it into small florets. If you want to use chicken, sub 2 cups (280 g) of cooked, shredded chicken for the cauliflower and skip the part in step 2 where you cook it for 10 minutes. Instead, place the chicken in the pan, season with garlic powder, salt, and pepper, cook for 2 minutes, and then proceed to step 3.

1 tablespoon olive oil

1 pound (454 g) riced cauliflower (about 4 cups)

1 teaspoon garlic powder

Kosher salt and freshly ground black pepper

2 tablespoons unsalted butter

½ cup (120 ml) buffalo-style hot sauce, like Frank's RedHot

4 ounces (113 g) cream cheese, cubed and softened

4 ounces (113 g) shredded Colby-Jack (about 1 cup)

¼ cup (55 g) sour cream

1 ounce (28 g) crumbled blue cheese (about ¼ cup; optional)

1 small celery stalk, thinly sliced on a bias

2 scallions, thinly sliced

Tortilla chips, potato chips, toasted baguette slices, celery sticks, and/or carrot sticks, for serving

1 Preheat the oven to 400°F (200°C).

2 Heat the olive oil in a large, deep skillet over medium-high heat. Add the cauliflower and garlic powder, and season with salt and pepper. Cook, stirring every couple minutes, until the cauliflower is browned and slightly caramelized, 10 to 12 minutes. The pan will be overcrowded at first, but that's okay.

3 Reduce the heat to low, add the butter and hot sauce, and stir to coat the cauliflower. Continue cooking for 1 minute to thicken and melt the butter.

4 Stir in the cream cheese until melted, and remove from the heat. Stir in half of the Colby-Jack and the sour cream.

5 Transfer the mixture to a 1-quart (1 L) baking dish, and sprinkle the top with the remaining Colby-Jack. Bake for about 10 minutes, until the cheese has melted and the dip is bubbling.

6 Remove from the oven, and sprinkle the top with the blue cheese (if using), thinly sliced celery, and scallions. Serve with the chips or baguette and/or vegetable sticks.

PREP AHEAD

Make the dip through step 4 up to 4 days in advance. Store in an airtight container in the fridge. When ready to eat, continue on with step 5 and 6. You may need to add a few minutes to the bake time.

SPINACH, ARTICHOKE, AND GREEN OLIVE DIP

serves 6 to 8 as a party snack

Here we take what might be the most classic dip—the beloved spinach artichoke dip—and turn it on its head by trading the traditional mozzarella for Gouda and adding smashed mild green olives. Call us crazy, but we like it better this way. Be sure to use a soft, young Gouda and mild green olives so as not to overwhelm the rest of the ingredients. Smash the olives with the flat side of your knife before chopping them to help break them down a little more. And serve this one hot, straight off the stovetop or after a blitz in the oven. If you find the dip to be thicker than you'd like in the end, thin it out with some buttermilk, milk, or even water. Start with 1 tablespoon and work your way up from there.

2 tablespoons olive oil

1 large garlic clove, grated

10 ounces (283 g) fresh baby spinach, roughly chopped (about 8 cups)

Kosher salt

One 14-ounce (397 g) can artichoke hearts, drained and roughly chopped

⅓ cup (50 g) pitted green olives, smashed and roughly chopped

8 ounces (227 g) cream cheese, cubed and softened

4 ounces (113 g) young Gouda, shredded

½ cup (110 g) Lime Crème Fraîche (page 41) or sour cream

¼ cup (27 g) finely grated Parmesan

Hot sauce (optional)

Tortilla chips or toasted baguette slices, for serving

1 Heat the oil in a large skillet over medium-high heat. Add the garlic, and cook for 30 seconds. Add as much spinach as will fit in the pan, and cook until it wilts, adding more spinach when there is room. Season with salt, and continue cooking until the spinach is wilted, about 2 minutes. Use a spatula to press the spinach against the side of the pan to release its water. While holding the spinach against one side of the pan, tilt the pan over the sink to pour out most of the water. Return the pan to the heat, and continue cooking until most of the remaining water has evaporated off, another 1 to 2 minutes.

2 Add the artichoke hearts and olives, and cook for 3 minutes to meld the flavors.

3 Reduce the heat to low, add the cream cheese and Gouda, and stir until melted and incorporated. Stir in the Lime Crème Fraîche and Parmesan, and season with salt and a few dashes of hot sauce (if using).

4 Serve as is, or to up the ante, transfer the dip to a 1-quart (1 L) baking dish and place it under the broiler for a few minutes, until the dip is browned and bubbling. Serve with chips or baguette slices and more hot sauce on the side.

PREP AHEAD

Make up to 4 days in advance. Store in an airtight container in the fridge. Reheat on the stove over medium-low heat or in a 350°F (180°C) oven until warmed through.

HACKABLE

You can sub frozen spinach for fresh. Be sure to thaw it and squeeze the liquid out of it before using.

MUSHROOM PÂTÉ

serves 8 as a party snack

Surprise, this is vegan! It's also one of Brie's go-to dinner party recipes. By combining an assortment of fancy mushrooms like trumpet, maitake, or hedgehog with a basic cremini or button variety, this country-style pâté takes on more complexity and deeper umami notes. Make a double recipe to use this in the Vegetables Wellington (page 154).

8 ounces (227 g) fancy mushrooms (trumpet, maitake, hedgehog, or your choice), woody ends trimmed and roughly chopped

8 ounces (227 g) cremini or button mushrooms, woody ends trimmed and roughly chopped

1 medium shallot, roughly chopped

1 small carrot, roughly chopped

1 small celery stalk, roughly chopped

¼ cup (60 ml) olive oil, plus more as needed

Kosher salt and freshly ground black pepper

2 garlic cloves, roughly chopped

½ teaspoon chopped fresh rosemary

½ cup (60 g) toasted walnut pieces

1 teaspoon aged balsamic vinegar

Toasted baguette slices or crackers, for serving

1 Preheat the oven to 400°F (200°C).

2 Combine the fancy and cremini mushrooms, shallot, carrot, and celery in a large bowl, and toss with the olive oil until evenly coated. Season liberally with salt and pepper.

3 Add the mixture to a large, rimmed baking sheet, and roast for about 30 minutes, until the mushrooms have browned and most of the water that they release has evaporated. Shake the pan and rotate it halfway through cooking.

4 Remove from the oven. Stir in the garlic and rosemary, and roast for another 5 minutes, until the garlic is fragrant. Remove from the oven, and let cool for 10 minutes.

5 Add the roasted mushroom mixture and the walnuts to a food processor, and pulse to a coarse, country-style pâté-like texture. The mixture should be quite chunky but easily spreadable onto a cracker. Transfer the pâté to a bowl.

6 Stir in the balsamic, and add more olive oil, 1 tablespoon at a time, if the mix seems dry. It should just hold together. Season with more salt, if needed.

7 Serve with the baguette slices or crackers.

SPECIAL EQUIPMENT
Food processor

PREP AHEAD
Make up to 4 days in advance. Store in an airtight container in the fridge. Best served slightly chilled or at room temperature.

A DIFFERENT TUNA HELPER

serves 6 to 8

This is not your mother's tuna noodle casserole. We omit the canned condensed soup and butter and go for a healthier, Mediterranean-style version with olive oil, capers, lemon, and olives. Make sure to use olive oil–packed tuna for best results. You can omit the Parmesan to make this fully dairy-free.

Butter or pan spray, for greasing

1 pound (454 g) orecchiette or pasta shells

½ cup (120 ml) olive oil

3 medium shallots, finely chopped

1 large carrot, finely chopped

Kosher salt and freshly ground black pepper

¾ cup (112 g) pitted green olives, smashed and roughly chopped

6 garlic cloves, thinly sliced

Zest of 1 lemon

½ teaspoon red pepper flakes

Three 5-ounce (142 g) cans tuna in olive oil, drained

One 14-ounce (397 g) can diced tomatoes

1 tablespoon chopped fresh oregano

4 ounces (113 g) Parmesan, finely grated (about 1 cup)

3 tablespoons roughly chopped fresh parsley

2 tablespoons fresh lemon juice

Fried Capers (page 36)

1 Preheat the oven to 350°F (180°C). Grease a 9 × 13-inch (23 × 33 cm) baking dish with butter or pan spray.

2 Bring a large pot of salted water to a boil over high heat. Add the pasta, and cook until 3 minutes shy of al dente. (It will finish cooking in the oven.) Reserve 2 cups (480 ml) of the pasta water and then drain the pasta and set it aside.

3 Wipe out the pot. Add the olive oil, and set the pot over medium heat. Add the shallots and carrot, and season with salt and pepper. Cook until they are soft but not browned, about 4 minutes.

4 Add the olives, garlic, lemon zest, and red pepper flakes, and cook for 2 more minutes.

5 Reduce the heat to low, stir in the tuna, and cook until it's broken down and well coated in oil, about 3 minutes. Use a wooden spoon to break the tuna up into small flakes as it cooks.

6 Add the tomatoes, the oregano, and the 2 cups (480 ml) reserved pasta water. Bring to a boil. Reduce the heat to low, and simmer for 5 minutes to meld the flavors. Season with salt.

7 Add the pasta to the pot, and stir until it's well coated in the tuna mixture. Add half of the Parmesan, half of the parsley, and the lemon juice, and stir to combine. Season with more salt, if needed. Transfer the pasta to the prepared baking dish, and top with the remaining Parmesan.

8 Bake for about 30 minutes, until browned and bubbling. Remove from the oven, top with the remaining parsley and the Fried Capers, and serve.

FREEZABLE

HACKABLE
Use fresh capers instead of fried. Sprinkle them on top of the dish before baking.

PREP AHEAD
Follow the instructions through step 7 and refrigerate for up to 3 days or freeze for up to 1 month. If frozen, thaw fully before baking, and continue with step 8. You will likely need to add 10 to 15 more minutes of bake time.

KING RANCH CASSEROLE

serves 6 to 8

King Ranch Casserole is a Texas mid-century potluck staple that's named after the largest ranch in the United States. King Ranch (the *actual* ranch, not the casserole) is more than 825,000 acres, which makes it bigger than Rhode Island. No one is sure why the dish is named after it, because the ranch had nothing to do with the development of the recipe. The most common iteration of King Ranch (the casserole, not the *actual* ranch) uses canned cream of mushroom soup. We mimic that flavor with fresh mushrooms instead. Its secret ingredient, Ro-Tel, is a Texas pantry staple of canned diced tomatoes and green chiles; it was made famous by Lady Bird Johnson in her Pedernales River Chili recipe. If you have trouble finding it, substitute one 14.5-ounce (411 g) can of diced tomatoes and one 4-ounce (113 g) can of diced green chiles.

1½ pounds (680 g) boneless, skinless chicken (breast, thigh, or a combo)

Kosher salt and freshly ground black pepper

Butter or pan spray, for greasing

4 tablespoons olive oil, divided

2 tablespoons unsalted butter

8 ounces (227 g) white button mushrooms, stems removed and finely chopped

1 yellow onion, diced into ¼-inch (6 mm) pieces

1 large jalapeño, seeded and diced into ¼-inch (6 mm) pieces

1 poblano, seeded and diced into ¼-inch (6 mm) pieces

4 large garlic cloves, thinly sliced

2 tablespoons all-purpose flour

1 tablespoon chili powder

2 teaspoons ground cumin

1 teaspoon garlic powder

One 10-ounce (283 g) can Ro-Tel

½ cup (120 ml) half-and-half

½ cup (110 g) sour cream

Twelve 6-inch (15 cm) corn tortillas, torn or cut into 2-inch (5 cm) pieces

8 ounces (227 g) Colby-Jack, shredded

FOR SERVING

Pico de Gallo (page 33) or finely chopped white onion

Lime Crème Fraîche (page 41) or sour cream

1 Preheat the oven to 350°F (180°C). Grease a 9 × 13-inch (23 × 33 cm) baking dish with butter or pan spray.

2 Season the chicken with salt, and add it to a large pot. Just cover it with water (4 to 6 cups/960 ml to 1.5 L should do) Set over medium-high heat, and bring to a boil. Reduce the heat to medium, and simmer, uncovered, until the chicken is just cooked through, 8 to 15 minutes, skimming the top of impurities as needed. Thighs and small breasts will cook more quickly than large, thick breasts, so use tongs to remove the chicken pieces from the pot separately, as they finish cooking; it may not all be done at the same time.

3 Transfer the cooked chicken to a large bowl, and continue to simmer the remaining broth on low until it has reduced to 2 cups (480 ml), 30 to 40 minutes. Strain the liquid through a fine-mesh strainer. Reserve 1 cup (240 ml) broth for this recipe, and save the other cup (240 ml) for whatever you want. You can store it in the fridge for up to 1 week or freeze it for a few months.

4 When the chicken is cool enough to handle, shred it into bite-size chunks, season with salt and pepper, and set aside.

5 Heat 2 tablespoons olive oil and the butter in a large skillet over medium-high heat. Add the mushrooms; the pan will be overcrowded, but that's okay. Season with salt and pepper, and cook until most of the water evaporates and the mushrooms just start to brown on the edges, 8 to 10 minutes. Transfer the mushrooms to the bowl with the chicken.

6 Add the remaining 2 tablespoons olive oil to the skillet. Add the onion, jalapeño, and poblano; season with salt; and continue to cook over medium-high heat until the vegetables become translucent and just start to brown, 5 to 7 minutes. Add the garlic, and cook for an additional minute.

7 Stir in the flour, chili powder, cumin, and garlic powder, and cook, stirring constantly, for 1 minute.

8 Reduce the heat to low, and stir in 1 cup (240 ml) of the reserved broth. Scrape up any darkened bits from the

bottom of the pan, and bring it to a simmer. Stir in the Ro-Tel and half-and-half, including the juices from the can, and continue to simmer for 2 to 3 minutes to thicken. Remove from the heat, and stir in the sour cream.

9   Reserve ⅓ cup (80 ml) of the sauce. Pour the rest into the bowl with the chicken and mushrooms, and stir to combine. Taste and season with more salt and pepper, if needed.

10   Spread the reserved ⅓ cup (80 ml) sauce on the bottom of the prepared baking dish. Evenly arrange half of the tortillas along the bottom, making sure the entire pan is covered; it's okay if there is some overlap and/or small gaps. Evenly spread half of the saucy chicken mixture over the tortillas, and top that with half of the shredded Colby-Jack. Spread the remaining tortillas evenly on top of the cheese and then finish with the remaining saucy chicken and the last of the Colby-Jack.

11   Bake for 25 to 30 minutes, until browned and bubbling. Remove from the oven, sprinkle the top with Pico de Gallo, and let cool for 10 minutes before slicing. Serve with the Lime Crème Fraîche on the side.

FREEZABLE

SPECIAL EQUIPMENT
Fine mesh strainer

HACKABLE
Substitute 3 cups (420 g) shredded store-bought rotisserie chicken and chicken stock for the chicken and the broth cooked in steps 2, 3, and 4.

PREP AHEAD
Follow the instructions through step 10, and refrigerate for up to 3 days or freeze for up to 1 month. If frozen, thaw fully before baking, and continue with step 11. You will likely need to add 10 to 15 more minutes of bake time.

Welcome!
Come on in...
★
the hot dogs
are waiting
ya!

BAKED ZITI ALL'ARRABBIATA ALLA VODKA À LA PARTY PEOPLE

serves 8

This isn't a clever name; it's what happens when a couple bona fide Party People upgrade the tried-and-true classic baked ziti into a new! and! improved! dish! We did so by marrying spicy arrabbiata with a mild and creamy vodka sauce and throwing in a dash of hot dogs. It took every ounce of strength Courtney had not to add an obscene amount of black pepper to this recipe.

3 tablespoons olive oil

1 yellow onion, finely chopped

Kosher salt and freshly ground black pepper

4 garlic cloves, thinly sliced

1 teaspoon red pepper flakes

One 1-pound (454 g) package hot dogs, sliced ¼-inch-thick (6 mm) on a bias

¾ cup (180 ml) vodka

One 28-ounce (794 g) can whole peeled tomatoes, crushed by hand, in their juices

One 14-ounce (397 g) can crushed tomatoes, fire roasted if possible

1 bay leaf

1 teaspoon dried oregano

¾ cup (180 ml) heavy cream

1 pound (454 g) ziti, rigatoni, or penne pasta

1 cup (227 g) whole milk ricotta

8 ounces (227 g) fresh mozzarella, torn into bite-size pieces

4 ounces (113 g) Parmesan, finely grated (about 1 cup)

1 Heat the olive oil in a large pot or deep skillet over medium heat. Add the onion, season with salt, and cook until translucent, about 5 minutes. Add the garlic and red pepper flakes, and cook for 1 minute. Add the hot dogs, and cook until browned, about 10 minutes.

2 Add the vodka, and continue cooking, scraping the bottom of the pan, until it has reduced by half, about 3 minutes. Stir in the whole peeled tomatoes, crushed tomatoes, bay leaf, and oregano, and bring to a simmer. Reduce the heat to a low simmer, and cook for 30 minutes, stirring occasionally.

3 Stir in the heavy cream, and remove from the heat. Remove that bay leaf while you're at it. Taste and season with more salt, if needed, and a generous (not obscene!) amount of black pepper.

4 While the sauce simmers, preheat the oven to 375°F (190°C) and bring a large pot of salted water to a boil over high heat. Add the pasta and boil until 3 minutes shy of al dente. (It will finish cooking in the oven.) Drain the pasta.

5 Return the pasta to the pot. Add the sauce, and toss until the pasta is well coated. It should be quite wet.

6 Pour half of the mixture into a 9 × 13-inch (23 × 33 cm) baking dish. Dollop half of the ricotta evenly over the top, followed by half of the mozzarella and half of the Parmesan. Pour the rest of the pasta mixture on top and then cover with the remaining cheeses.

7 Bake for 20 to 25 minutes, until the cheeses are melty and browned, and the sauce begins bubbling up around the edges. Remove from the oven, and let it sit for a few minutes before serving.

FREEZABLE

NOTE
This works with any type of sausage (kielbasa, bratwurst, etc.), not just hot dogs.

PREP AHEAD
Follow the instructions through step 6, and refrigerate for up to 3 days or freeze for up to 1 month. If frozen, thaw fully before baking, and continue with step 7. You will likely need to add 10 to 15 more minutes of bake time.

CHICKEN SPAGHETTI

serves 8

You may read the ingredients here and think, "Hey, this is awfully similar to King Ranch casserole." And you are correct, sort of. The ingredients are quite alike, but the dishes are a world apart in vibe. Chicken Spaghetti has been around since the sixties. It's a Southern dish—a cheesier, baked cousin of tetrazzini. Admittedly, it's a boring name for something bursting with this much flavor: We boil the spaghetti in chicken broth, for God's sake. Talk about toothsome! Like with many of the other casseroles in this book, we omit the oft-used condensed soup in favor of freshly sautéed mushrooms and a béchamel-esque sauce. If you have trouble finding Ro-Tel, substitute one 14.5-ounce (411 g) can of diced tomatoes and one 4-ounce (113 g) can of diced green chiles.

Butter or pan spray, for greasing

1½ pounds (680 g) boneless, skinless chicken (breast, thigh, or a combo)

Kosher salt and freshly ground black pepper

8 ounces (227 g) spaghetti, broken into thirds

4 tablespoons unsalted butter

8 ounces (227 g) white button mushrooms, stems removed and finely chopped

2 celery stalks, finely chopped

1 large green chile (poblano, Anaheim, hatch, or bell pepper), seeded and finely chopped

1 yellow onion, finely chopped

4 garlic cloves, thinly sliced

2½ tablespoons all-purpose flour

½ teaspoon garlic powder

½ teaspoon onion powder

1 cup (240 ml) whole milk

One 10-ounce (283 g) can Ro-Tel

8 ounces (227 g) cheddar, grated (about 2 cups), divided

6 ounces (165 g) Parmesan, finely grated (about 1½ cups)

1 Preheat the oven to 350°F (180°C). Grease a 9 × 13-inch (23 × 33 cm) baking dish with butter or pan spray.

2 Season the chicken with salt, and add it to a large pot. Just cover it with water (4 to 6 cups/960 ml to 1.5 L should do). Set over medium-high heat, and bring to a boil. Reduce the heat to medium, and simmer until the chicken is just cooked through, 8 to 15 minutes, skimming the top of impurities as needed. Thighs and small breasts will cook more quickly than large, thick breasts, so use tongs to remove the chicken pieces from the pot separately, as they finish cooking; it may not all be done at the same time.

3 Place the cooked chicken in a large bowl. Reserve 1½ cups (360 ml) of the broth, and set it aside. When the chicken is cool enough to handle, shred it into bite-size chunks, and season it with more salt and pepper, if needed.

4 Meanwhile, add enough water to the remaining chicken broth in the pot to make 4 cups (960 ml). Season it with more salt, if needed, and bring to a boil over high heat. Add the spaghetti, and cook it until 5 minutes shy of al dente, about 6 minutes for most pasta brands. There won't be as much liquid in the pot as you are probably used to boiling pasta in. It's okay. You'll just need to stir the pasta more often to make sure it doesn't stick together. Drain the pasta, reserving ¼ cup (60 ml) of the pasta cooking liquid, and transfer it to a large bowl.

5 Heat the butter in a large, deep skillet or pot over medium-high heat. Add the mushrooms and cook until browned, 4 to 5 minutes. Add the celery, green chile, and onion, and season with salt. Cook for an additional 5 minutes, until the onions are translucent.

6 Add the garlic, and cook for 1 minute. Stir in the flour, garlic powder, and onion powder, and cook, stirring constantly, for 1 minute.

7 Reduce the heat to low, and slowly stir in the milk and the reserved 1½ cups (360 ml) chicken broth. Scape the bottom of the pan, and stir constantly so it doesn't get lumpy. Stir in the Ro-Tel, including the juices, bring to a simmer, and cook for 2 minutes to thicken.

8 Add the chicken and season with more salt, if needed. Remove from the heat.

9 Toss the mixture with the spaghetti, half of the cheddar, and the Parmesan. Taste and add more salt and pepper, if needed. If the mixture seems dry, add up to ¼ cup (60 ml) of the reserved pasta cooking liquid. Spread the mixture evenly in the prepared baking dish, and top with the rest of the cheddar.

10 Bake for about 30 minutes, until the cheese melts and the sauce is bubbling. Remove from the oven, and let cool for a few minutes before serving.

FREEZABLE

PREP AHEAD
Follow the instructions through step 9 and refrigerate for up to 3 days or freeze for up to 1 month. If frozen, thaw fully before baking, and continue on with step 10. You will likely need to add 10 to 15 more minutes of bake time.

HACKABLE
Substitute 3 cups (420 g) shredded store-bought rotisserie chicken and chicken stock for the chicken and the broth cooked in steps 2 through 4.

SOUTHERN MAC 'N' CHEESE

serves 8

Opinions abound on whether baked or stovetop mac is better, and while there is no such thing as bad mac 'n' cheese, we definitely lean toward the kind that's baked, especially when it's topped with a plethora of Garlic Toast Crunchies (page 37). And that's pretty much everything we have to say about the subject.

Butter or pan spray, for greasing

1 pound (454 g) large elbow noodles

8 ounces (227 g) mild cheddar, grated (about 2 cups)

8 ounces (227 g) sharp cheddar, grated (about 2 cups)

4 ounces (113 g) Colby-Jack, grated (about 1 cup)

4 tablespoons unsalted butter

⅓ cup (46 g) all-purpose flour

4 cups (960 ml) whole milk

⅔ cup (160 ml) buttermilk

⅔ cup (160 ml) heavy cream

Kosher salt and freshly ground black pepper

Freshly grated nutmeg

Garlic Toast Crunchies (page 37; optional but highly recommended)

1 Preheat the oven to 375°F (190°C). Grease a 9 × 13-inch (23 × 33 cm) baking dish with butter or pan spray.

2 Bring a large pot of heavily salted water to a boil over high heat. Add the noodles, and cook until 2 minutes shy of al dente. (They will finish cooking in the oven.) Drain the pasta, and set it aside.

3 Combine the mild and sharp cheddars and the Colby-Jack in a large bowl. Reserve 1 cup (113 g) of the cheese mixture, and set it aside.

4 Wipe out the pot. Add the butter, and set over medium heat. Add the flour, and cook, stirring constantly, for about 1 minute. The flour shouldn't brown; just cook the rawness out of it.

5 Slowly add the milk, buttermilk, and heavy cream while whisking constantly. Bring the mixture to a high simmer over medium-high heat while whisking or stirring often to avoid clumps.

6 Reduce the heat to low. Add the cheese mixture, and stir until it has melted and incorporated, about 1 minute. Turn off the heat. Season the cheese sauce with salt, pepper, and several grates of nutmeg and then stir in the pasta. If it seems thin, or like there's too much of it, that's okay—we want it that way. It will thicken as it bakes, silly!

7 Transfer the mac mixture to the baking dish, sprinkle the top with the reserved 1 cup (113 g) of the cheese mixture, and top with the Garlic Toast Crunchies (if using).

8 Bake until lightly browned on top and bubbling, about 30 minutes.

FREEZABLE

PREP AHEAD
Follow the instructions through step 7 and refrigerate for up to 3 days or freeze for up to 1 month. If frozen, thaw fully before baking, and continue on with step 8. You will likely need to add 10 to 15 more minutes of bake time.

RATATOUILLE

Serves 6 to 8

This recipe is another one of our surprise vegan numbers. It's important to bake each vegetable on a separate sheet pan, not only because they cook at different rates but also to allow for sufficient browning via not overcrowding the pan, which is crucial to this dish's flavor development. If you can't fit all four sheet pans in the oven at once, hold off on salting any veggies that are left out until just before you put them in the oven. The salt will cause them to release moisture, which will turn into steam and make it harder for them to brown. Use bell, cubanelle, or Jimmy Nardello for the sweet red peppers.

4 yellow squash or zucchini or a mix (about 1½ pounds/680 g), sliced into ¼-inch (6 mm) rounds

2 medium eggplants (about 1½ pounds/680 g), sliced into 1-inch (2.5 cm) cubes

2 yellow onions (about 1 pound/454 g), halved and sliced into ½-inch (1 cm) strips

2 sweet red peppers (about ½ pound/227 g), sliced into ¼-inch (6 mm) strips

13 tablespoons olive oil, divided

Kosher salt and freshly ground black pepper

3 garlic cloves, roughly chopped

½ teaspoon red pepper flakes (optional)

One 28-ounce (794 g) can whole peeled tomatoes, crushed by hand, in their juices

1 teaspoon chopped fresh oregano, marjoram, or thyme

1 bay leaf

1 loaf crusty French bread

1 Preheat the oven to 350°F (180°C).

2 Spread the zucchini, eggplant, onions, and peppers onto four separate rimmed baking sheets. Toss the vegetables on each sheet with 3 tablespoons of olive oil and season with salt.

3 Add the pans to the oven, working in batches if they don't all fit, and cook until the vegetables are tender and just starting to brown on the edges, about 35 minutes for the peppers and onions, and 1 hour for the squash and eggplant. Give the squash and eggplant a stir halfway through cooking.

4 While the vegetables roast, make the tomato sauce: Heat the remaining 1 tablespoon olive oil in a medium pot over medium heat. Add the garlic and red pepper flakes (if using), and cook until fragrant, about 1 minute. Don't let that garlic burn!

5 Add the tomatoes, herbs, and bay leaf; season with salt and pepper; and bring to a simmer. Reduce the heat to low, and simmer for 15 minutes to meld the flavors. Remove the bay leaf.

6 Toss the roasted vegetables and the tomato sauce together in a large bowl. Season with more salt and pepper, if needed, and transfer the mixture to a 9 × 13-inch (23 × 33 cm) baking dish.

7 Bake for about 1 hour, stirring halfway through, until the vegetables become super soft and melty. If you'd like the vegetables to be saucier, add up to ½ cup (120 ml) water or vegetable stock to the pan when you stir it at the halfway point. Serve warm or at room temperature, with that crusty bread on the side.

PREP AHEAD
Make this up to 3 days in advance. Store in the fridge, and reheat in a 350°F (180°C) oven until warmed through.

game night

menu

Aviation (page 53), Cheesy Jenga Bread (page 79), French Onion Ramen Dip (page 121), Ratatouille (page 138), Cheese Danish Galette (page 110). Add on The Simplest of Salads (page 166), if desired.

ambiance

Keep the lights high enough so people can see what they are doing, but not so high that it's unflattering (the horror!). Be sure to have an appropriately sized table or area for where the game(s) will take place and seats for everyone, if applicable. Streamers, as always, are a nice touch.

dress

Cute, casual, and easy to move around in, in case someone busts out Twister.

playlist suggestions

Throw some classic Nintendo and game show theme songs in the mix, plus any songs with names that are "game-related": "Games People Play" by the Alan Parsons Project, "Foolish Games" by Jewel, "Pinball Wizard" by The Who, "Games Without Frontiers" by Peter Gabriel, "Video Games" by Lana Del Rey, "Games" by The Strokes, "Wicked Game" by Chris Isaac.

Game nights are classics for a reason; the main reason is that they are so much fun. The games can be anything: Board games, card games, drinking games, bingo, and charades are all super choices. Another option is to order vintage games online; there are some *really* weird ones from the seventies and eighties. Or you can even make up your own game. A friend of Courtney's created one called Dice Party that is a cross between musical chairs, dice throwing, and a white elephant gift exchange, but with gifts people actually want. It's a hoot. What we are trying to say is, Game Night is only as wild and vast as your imagination will allow it to be.

prep plan

two days out: Make the shallots for the deviled eggs; make the Aviation base; make the Ratatouille.

one day out: Make the deviled eggs through step 4; make the Tonnato for the deviled eggs; make the dip; set up decorations (if using); stage serving utensils, platters, plates, and napkins; set up as much of the bar area as possible.

morning of the party: Make the galette; make the Cheesy Jenga Bread through step 7.

as guests arrive: Set out the Aviations and ice at the bar area; assemble and serve the deviled eggs; serve the dip; bake and serve the Cheesy Jenga Bread.

during the party: Reheat and serve the Ratatouille; make and serve the salad (if using); serve the galette.

relaxing karaoke

Relaxing karaoke is a staple in the Larson and McBroom households. The premise is simple: Wear your coziest clothes, gather your favorite at-home spa products, and laze around with your pals while you take turns singing karaoke and giving each other facials. Although it's a nice touch, you don't need a karaoke machine or microphone to pull this off. Just google the songs + "karaoke version" and belt them out with your natural singing voice.

menu

Party People Punch (PPP; page 50), Party People Pepperoni Pizza Pockets (PPPPP; page 88), Buffalo Cauliflower Dip (page 122), Southern Mac 'n' Cheese (page 137), Party People Pop-Tart Peach Pie (PPP-TPP; page 106). Add on The Simplest of Salads (page 166), if desired.

prep plan

three days out: Make the punch base, including the Chile Lime Salt; make the garlic crumbs for the mac 'n' cheese (if using).

two days out: Make the pizza pockets through step 5.

one day out: Make the buffalo dip through step 4 and the mac 'n' cheese through step 7; set up decorations (if using); stage serving utensils, platters, plates, and napkins; set up as much of the bar area as possible.

morning of the party: Make the peach pie.

as guests arrive: Set out the punch and ice at the bar area; bake the pizza pockets, warm the dipping sauce, and serve; bake and serve the buffalo dip.

during the party: Bake and serve the mac 'n' cheese; make and serve the salad (if using); serve the peach pie.

ambiance

Low light, lots of pillows and blankets, hot tea to lubricate those vocal cords, and pitchers of spa water with sliced cucumbers.

dress

The cozier, the better.

playlist suggestions

You don't need a playlist for this party, silly. The party *is* the playlist.

powerpoint party

We bet you have a ton of knowledge to share with your friend group, as they probably do with you. Since knowledge is power, let's take advantage of that. Tell each willing participant to create a slideshow about their favorite subject. It does not need to be even remotely professional. In fact, the sillier, the better. Each person gets five minutes to present to the group, and everyone walks away having learned something new. No subject is off the table—Blue Zones, the existence of Bigfoot, how to slay at puppeteering in three easy steps—anything goes. You'll need something to present from. We usually screen-mirror from a computer or phone onto a television set (it's the easiest move), but if you have an old-school projector, even better.

menu

Frozen Margs (aka Margarita Slush; page 63), Party People Mix (PP Mix; page 71), Chile con Queso (a Love Story; page 118), King Ranch Casserole (page 130), Candy Cherry Ritz Cake (page 100). Add on The Simplest of Salads (page 166), if desired.

prep plan

two days out: Make the frozen marg base through step 5 (if blending) or through step 2 (if using a slushie machine); make the party mix; make the Ritz cake through step 12.

one day out: Make the casserole through step 10; make the queso, including any extra mix-ins you want to add; make the Ritz frosting and frost the cake; set up decorations (if using); stage serving utensils, platters, plates, and napkins; set up as much of the bar area as possible.

as guests arrive: Pull the Ritz cake from the fridge to bring to room temperature; slush and serve the margs; put out the party mix; reheat the queso and serve.

during the party: Bake and serve the casserole; make and serve the salad (if using); slice and serve the Ritz cake.

dress

Power suits or casual Friday dress code encouraged.

ambiance

Fun office vibes, with lots of Post-it notes and memos. Everyone drinks out of coffee mugs. Don't forget to provide a water cooler to gossip around and a comment box for anonymous party feedback that HR can review later.

playlist suggestions

Go heavy on the power ballads and anything that refers to work or money: "Wind of Change" by Scorpions, "Shadows of the Night" by Pat Benatar, "Purple Rain" by Prince, "9 to 5" by Dolly Parton, "Workin' Man Blues" by Merle Haggard, "Hustlin'" by Rick Ross, and "Money" by Leikeli47.

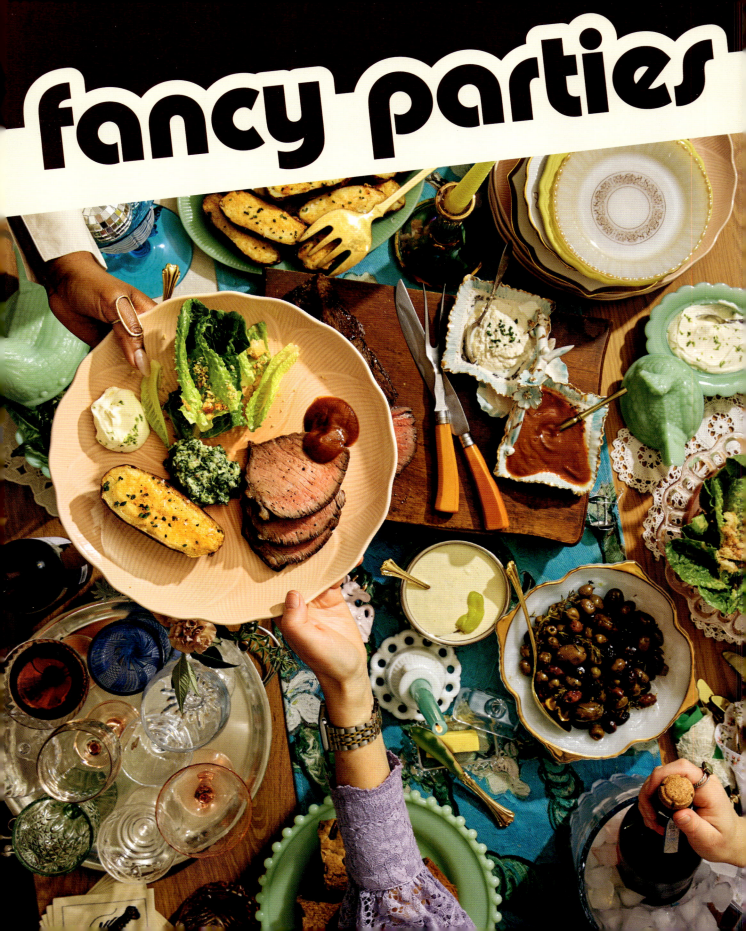

fancy parties

When compared to their casual cousins (see page 116), fancy parties are much more formal affairs. That's not to say everyone should roll up in their finest tuxedos and gowns, although they can if they want to (and if they are a Topper (see page 17), they probably will). It's just that the food takes a bit longer to prep, and it's best served to those seated at a proper dining room table. This chapter is divided into three parts: showstopping mains, big salads, and sides. The showstopping mains are all "large-format roasts"—hunks of meat or veggies that are cooked in the oven. The big salads and sides are exactly what they sound like. For your fancy party, you'll choose a main, a salad, and a side or two from this chapter and then add on a libation, a couple party snacks, and a dessert from the Party Essentials section (page 45). Serve the cocktail and party snacks as soon as your guests arrive and then move everyone to the dinner table for the main event. We like to serve the meal family style, because although we are certainly fancy, we are rarely fancy enough to individually plate everyone's food. Also, who has time for that? It's a good idea to grab a crusty loaf of bread and some fancy butter or olive oil for the table, too. Or pick up one of those grocery store garlic breads that come in the foil pouch (so good!). Be sure to offer beer or wine, and to really fancy it up, grab a yummy amaro or digestif for after dinner.

Fancy parties naturally lend themselves to milestone celebrations like anniversaries, birthdays, weddings, graduations, and other congratulatory events, but you know how we like an activity, so here's a few we'd like to offer up for the occasion.

fancy party activities

The Brag and Complain (you simply brag and/or complain while everyone listens and validates you)

Party Bowl (grab a bowl, set it in the middle of the dinner table, and ask guests to add questions to the bowl; when the moment strikes during dinner, people draw from the bowl and answer the question)

Friendly Debate Club (everyone comes prepared with a soapbox and speaking points to defend a position on something controversial, like whether a fox is actually a dog or a cat, for example)

fancy party ambiance and dress

These are bigger-deal celebrations, and the ambiance can be subdued or over the top. As the host, you get to make that decision. Don't forget that flattering, dim lighting is always best, but anything goes when it comes to streamers, balloons, confetti, party hats, disco balls, and everything in between. As far as getting dressed, use this as an excuse to don that outfit you always wanted to wear but never had the occasion for, or the one that feels a little too weird to be caught in public in.

DUELING ROAST CHICKENS

serves 8 to 10

Unfortunately, they don't make chickens big enough to feed a group larger than four or five. That's what turkeys are for. We assume you don't want to roast a turkey, so here's a recipe for two chickens instead. We unlocked the perfect procedure: Each chicken is salted overnight and then slathered in its own special flavor of butter—miso or ranch—before getting roasted slow and low, almost like a rotisserie. You barely have to think about them when they're in the oven, except to baste them, which is fun because it feels like painting. The butters should be extremely soft so they spread adequately, and don't worry about putting any of it under the skin (all that does is loosen up the skin to shrink in the oven, which results in naked, dried-out meat). Which chicken will reign supreme is anyone's guess, but it also doesn't matter. We combine each of their juices in the end to make one triumphant sauce. It's a symbol. The dueling chickens have overcome adversity, and unity and togetherness have won again.

2 whole chickens, 4 to 5 pounds (1.8 to 2.3 kg) each, patted dry

Kosher salt

¼ cup (58 g) Miso Butter (page 42), softened

1 teaspoon fish sauce

4 tablespoons unsalted butter, softened

2 teaspoons Ramen Ranch Seasoning (page 43)

1 lemon, halved

SPECIAL EQUIPMENT
Cooling rack

PREP AHEAD
Salt the chicken the night before.

NOTE
To carve a bird, start with the thighs and legs. Slice each thigh-leg combo off the body as a single unit, right through the skin and through the joint at the base of the thigh, and then cut through the joint between the thigh and the leg. Next, do the breasts. Slice downward at a slight angle along both sides of the breastbone. You can then slice the breasts into pieces or leave them whole. Cut off the wings next by slicing through the joint that connects them to the body and then use your hands to pull any extra meat off of what's left of the chicken. Be sure to flip it over and pick the meat off the back, too, especially the oysters, which live toward the rear. There are countless videos on the internet on how to carve a chicken if you are confused or need more direction than this.

1 Season the chickens liberally with salt, inside and out. Set a cooling rack over a rimmed baking sheet, and place the chickens on top. (If you don't have a cooling rack, you can place them directly on the baking sheet.) Refrigerate uncovered overnight.

2 Preheat the oven to 300°F (150°C). If you have a convection oven, make sure the convection is off.

3 Mix the Miso Butter and fish sauce in a small bowl.

4 Mix the unsalted butter and Ramen Ranch Seasoning in a separate small bowl.

5 Slather the Miso Butter all over one of the chickens and inside the cavity. Use the butter as glue to stick the wing tips to the sides of the breasts. Do the same thing with the ramen ranch butter on the other chicken.

6 Stuff each chicken with a lemon half, and place each of them on a separate rimmed baking sheet or in an ovenproof skillet.

7 Roast for 2½ to 3 hours, basting every hour, until golden brown and oh so tender.

8 Tilt the chickens so all the juices run out of the cavities and onto the baking sheets and then transfer the chickens to a large cutting board to rest for 20 minutes.

9 While the chickens rest, transfer all of their juices and pan drippings to a small pot. Or, if you roasted them in skillets, marry the juices into one of the pans. Finagle the lemons out of the chicken cavities, and squeeze the juice into the pan drippings. Set over medium-high heat, and bring to a boil. Reduce the heat to medium and simmer, whisking constantly, for 5 minutes to thicken.

10 Carve the chickens (see Note), and drizzle some of the buttery pan sauce over the tops. Serve the rest of the butter sauce on the side, for more drizzling.

A ROAST BEEF FOR US ALL

Serves 6 to 8

This was originally supposed to be a recipe for prime rib. But then came time to test it. You can't get a prime rib to feed eight people for less than $300—at least, not in LA. That's . . . not the vibe of this book. We needed to find an affordable option to feed a crowd. Enter chuck roast, commonly used for stews and slow braises. The butcher assured us that it would slap, so we got one and tested it out. It did slap, but not in a good way. In fact, it was awful. On to the next cut: the bottom round roast. Do you have *any* idea how hard it is to find a bottom round roast (and/or a rump roast) in the city of Los Angeles? At the time of this writing, it's dang near impossible. So we moved on to top sirloin, baby!! Coming in at a fraction of the price of prime rib, it roasted nicely and was full of flavor without being tough and gristly. Now this, *this* was a roast beef for us all. (Tri-tip or picanha would be great options, too, as they are both cuts taken from the sirloin.) Have the butcher truss it for you; it should be close to the same thickness throughout for even cooking. The secret to success is the reverse-sear method, which is how we'd cook any other cut, including prime rib. All this means is that you'll roast the meat at a low temperature until it hits your desired doneness—we suggest no more than medium—and then let it rest before browning it in the oven for a few minutes at the highest temperature possible. This ensures an evenly cooked roast with a nicely browned crust, and it's great for dinner parties, because you can roast it in advance so all you'll need to do is blast it in the oven before serving. It's best to slice this roast thinly, no thicker than ¼ inch (6 mm). And yes, you will need a meat thermometer. Serve the roast with Swayze Sauce (page 42), Pepperoncini Aioli (page 40), or Lime Crème Fraîche (page 41), and prepared horseradish for true steakhouse vibes.

One 3- to 4-pound (1.4 to 1.8 kg) top sirloin roast, trussed

Kosher salt and freshly ground black pepper

FOR SERVING

Swayze Sauce (page 42)

Pepperoncini Aioli (page 40)

Lime Crème Fraîche (page 41)

Prepared horseradish

PREP AHEAD

Cook the roast up to 2 days in advance, through step 3. Wrap and store it in the fridge. Remove the roast from the fridge 2 hours before you plan to reheat it. Reheat it, uncovered, in a 225°F (110°C) oven until just warmed through, about 1 hour, before proceeding with steps 4 and 5.

SPECIAL EQUIPMENT

Cooling rack and meat thermometer

1 Place a rack on a rimmed baking sheet. Season the roast generously with salt. (We mean it: Use a lot of salt. Like, use at least 1 tablespoon of salt.) Place the roast on the rack, and throw that sucker in the fridge overnight. Don't cover it. She needs to dry out. Remove the roast from the fridge 2 hours before you plan to cook it.

2 Preheat the oven to 225°F (110°C). Pat the roast dry, and season it with some pepper. Keep it on the rack, and roast it until an instant read thermometer registers 115°F to 120°F (46°C to 49°C) for medium rare or 125°F to 130°F (52°C to 54°C) for medium, about 2½ to 3½ hours, depending on the size of your roast. (Keep in mind that the temperature will rise about 10°F/6°C after resting.)

3 Remove from the oven, and tent the roast loosely with foil. Allow it to rest for at least 30 minutes and up to 1 hour.

4 Crank the oven up as high as it will go while you're waiting. We're looking at you, 500°F to 550°F (260°C to 288°C)! Remove the foil and throw the roast back in the oven for 5 to 8 minutes, watching it closely, until it's dark brown and crispy.

5 Remove from the oven, undo the trussing, slice, and serve immediately (no need to rest again) with the Swayze Sauce, Pepperoncini Aioli, Lime Crème Fraîche, and prepared horseradish.

KALUA PORK

Serves 8

Slow-roasted pork butt is the easiest way to feed a group of people, every time. Variations of this pork cookery method exist in most cultures. Here, we head to Hawaii, where they use an underground oven called an imu and roast the pork over hot coals and banana leaves, which results in earthy, smoky, succulent, fall-apart-tender meat. We aren't about to tell you to dig an imu in your yard. (But also, maybe you should?) You can mimic the flavor by wrapping the pork in a banana leaf and adding a few drops of liquid smoke. It's not the same, but it's mighty tasty. Banana leaves are often found in the freezer section of the grocery store, and they are also available online. Be sure to defrost them before using. If you can't find banana leaves, it's okay to omit them. Serve the pork with any combination of the following: Chow Chow (page 31), Swayze Sauce (page 42), sriracha mayo, Comeback Sauce (page 40), Pepperoncini Aioli (page 40), Coconut Lime Rice Pilaf (page 177), Hawaiian rolls, plain rice, or lettuce for making wraps.

5 pounds (2.3 kg) boneless pork butt

Kosher salt and freshly ground black pepper

2 tablespoons canola, vegetable, or grapeseed oil (or shallot oil; page 35)

Banana leaf

3 tablespoons sugar

1 tablespoon liquid smoke

Assorted condiments, rolls, rice, and/or lettuce (see Headnote), for serving

1 Preheat the oven to 325°F (165°C).

2 Pat the pork dry, and season generously with salt and pepper.

3 Heat the oil in a large ovenproof pot or Dutch oven over medium-high heat. When the oil starts to get wavy, add the pork and sear on all sides until browned, 2 to 3 minutes per side. Transfer the pork to a plate.

4 Deglaze the pan with ½ cup (120 ml) water, use a wooden spoon or spatula to scrape up any browned bits from the bottom of the pan, and then turn off the heat.

5 Open a large banana leaf, and carefully place it in the bottom of the pan so the leaf covers the bottom and comes up the sides. Place the seared pork in the center of the leaf. Sprinkle the top with the sugar, and drizzle it with the liquid smoke. Fold the banana leaf over the pork to make a packet. It's okay if the leaf doesn't fully cover the pork.

6 Cover the pot, and braise in the oven for 4 to 5 hours, until the pork is super soft and falling apart. Remove from the oven, and let cool.

7 When the pork is cool enough to handle, remove the banana leaf and shred the pork in its juices. Serve with the condiments and accompaniments of your choice.

FREEZABLE

PREP AHEAD
Store the cooked, shredded pork in the fridge for up to 4 days or in the freezer for up to 1 month. Thaw before using. Reheat in a 325°F (165°C) oven, covered, until warmed though.

SALSA VERDE SNAPPER

Serves 6 to 8

Many people are intimidated by a whole fish, but y'all are gonna flip when you realize how easy this is to make. The recipe is very much based on the coastal Mexican method of smothering fish in salsa and grilling it to perfection, called "a la talla." Our version is designed to roast in the oven at very high heat, but you could grill it if you like. Do so over medium-high coals with the skin-side down until charred, about 7 minutes. Flip and grill the other side for 3 to 4 minutes. Use a fish grilling basket for a regret-free experience. Plan for about 3 tortillas per person, and if you're like us, pan-fry them in a little bit of oil first for added crunch. If snapper doesn't do it for you, or if you have trouble sourcing it, use trout or branzino instead. Ask your fishmonger to butterfly the fish for you, which is essentially removing the backbone and splaying both sides of the fish flat, like the wings of a butterfly. It's okay to make this recipe with more than one fish; you just need about 3 pounds (1.4 kg) in all.

1 cup (40 g) roughly chopped fresh Italian parsley or cilantro, or a combo

3 garlic cloves, smashed

½ cup (120 ml) olive oil

1½ tablespoons fresh lime juice

½ teaspoon ground cumin

Kosher salt

One whole red snapper (about 3 pounds/ 1.4 kg), scaled, deboned, and butterflied (head on or off)

Chile Lime Salt (page 36)

Small corn tortillas (street taco size)

FOR SERVING

Pico de Gallo (page 33) or salsa

Lime Crème Fraîche (page 41) or sour cream

1 Preheat the oven to 450°F (230°C). Line a rimmed baking sheet with foil.

2 Add the herbs, garlic, olive oil, lime juice, and cumin to a blender, and blend to a puree. Season with salt, and set aside.

3 Rinse and dry the fish, and place it skin-side down on the baking sheet. Season it liberally with the Chile Lime Salt and then spoon half (about ⅓ cup/75 g) of the salsa verde over the top. Reserve the rest of the sauce for serving.

4 Roast for 5 to 7 minutes, until the fish is just starting to turn opaque, and then turn the broiler to high and continue broiling for another 3 to 5 minutes, until the fish is lightly browned in places.

5 While the fish roasts, stack the tortillas: Wet your fingers and flick a little bit of water on top of each tortilla before stacking another on top. Wrap them in foil and set them in the oven to warm for about 5 minutes. (If the broiler is on when you place them in the oven, put them on the rack that's farthest away from the broiler.)

6 Serve the fish directly on the pan, or use the foil to transfer it to a large platter. Sprinkle the top with more Chile Lime Salt and some Pico de Gallo, and serve with extra pico, tortillas, Lime Crème Fraîche, and extra salsa verde on the side.

SPECIAL EQUIPMENT
Blender

PREP AHEAD
Make the salsa verde up to 2 weeks in advance. Store in an airtight container in the fridge.

HACKABLE
Substitute sour cream for the crème fraîche, store-bought salsa for the pico, and plain kosher salt for the Chile Lime Salt.

VEGETABLES WELLINGTON

Serves 8 to 10

This is the most labor-intensive recipe in the book, but all of the components can be made in advance, and the result is absolutely worth it. One of the main components is the Mushroom Pâté (page 126). You will need to double that recipe to have enough to use here. When you do, divide the mushrooms between two separate sheet pans in step 3. Be sure to use a serrated knife to slice the finished product; it will cut much more cleanly that way. If you use a dairy-free puff pastry, this recipe is vegan.

CURRIED LENTILS

2 tablespoons olive oil

1 medium leek, finely chopped

Kosher salt

½ teaspoon curry powder

¾ cup (160 g) dried red lentils

3 cups (720 ml) vegetable stock

Kosher salt and freshly ground black pepper

BUTTERNUT SQUASH

One 2- to 2½-pound (907 g to 1.1 kg) butternut squash

2 tablespoons olive oil

Kosher salt

TO ASSEMBLE

14 to 19 ounces (397 to 539 g) puff pastry, thawed

All-purpose flour, for dusting

2 batches Mushroom Pâté (page 126)

1 egg, beaten with 1 teaspoon water

VEGAN GRAVY

2 tablespoons olive oil

2 tablespoons all-purpose flour

2 cups (480 ml) vegetable stock

1 teaspoon Dijon mustard

3 fresh thyme sprigs

1 bay leaf

Kosher salt and freshly ground black pepper

1 Prepare the lentils: Heat the olive oil in a medium pot over medium-high heat. Add the leek, season with salt, and cook until softened, about 6 minutes. Add the curry powder, and cook for 1 minute. Add the lentils, and stir in the vegetable stock. Bring to a boil and then reduce the heat to a low simmer. Cook, uncovered and stirring occasionally, until the lentils are soft and all the stock has been absorbed, about 20 minutes. You should be able to drag a spoon through the bottom of the pot and leave a clear streak with no liquid seeping out. If after 20 minutes the lentils are cooked but a lot of liquid remains in the pot, crank up the heat to cook it off, stirring often. (Don't worry, you can't overcook the lentils.) If the lentils begin to dry out before they are soft, add more stock or water, ¼ cup (60 ml) at a time. Let the liquid absorb before adding more. Remove from the heat, season with salt and pepper, and cool to room temperature.

2 Prepare the butternut squash: Preheat the oven to 450°F (230°C). Peel and seed the butternut squash, and cut it into sticks about ½ inch (1 cm) wide × ½ inch (1 cm) tall × 4 inches (10 cm) long. Place them on a large, rimmed baking sheet, toss them with the olive oil, and season with salt. Roast for about 30 minutes, until browned. Use tongs to flip them over halfway through cooking. Remove from the oven, and reduce the temperature to 400°F (200°C).

3 Assemble the Wellington: Unfold the puff pastry onto a lightly floured piece of parchment paper. Use a rolling pin to roll it into a 12 × 16-inch (30 × 40 cm) rectangle and then transfer the parchment and the pastry to a large, rimmed baking sheet.

4 With the long (16-inch/40 cm) side facing you, spread the curried lentils over the left two-thirds of the puff pastry, leaving a 1-inch (2.5 cm) border on the left side, top, and bottom. (The right side will have a 5-inch/15 cm "border.") Spread 2 cups (266 g) of the Mushroom Pâté on top of the lentils. Arrange the butternut squash vertically on top of the mushrooms. Spread 1½ cups (200 g) of the Mushroom Pâté in a 3-inch (7.5 cm) mound right down the middle of the lentils/mushrooms/squash.

5 Fold the left side of the puff pastry (the one that's covered with filling) over the top of the mushroom mound you just created. If the pastry is too soft and hard to manage, throw it in the

SPECIAL EQUIPMENT

Rolling pin

PREP AHEAD

The lentils, squash, and Mushroom Pâté can be made up to 4 days in advance. Store each in a separate airtight container in the fridge. Bring each one to room temperature before assembling the Wellington. The gravy can be made up to 4 days in advance. Store in an airtight container in the fridge, and heat it before serving.

freezer for 5 to 10 minutes. Brush the top with some beaten egg, then fold the right side (aka the naked side) of the puff pastry over the top, stretching it, if needed, so it completely covers the entire pastry, all the way to the edge of the baking sheet. Fold the short ends of the puff pastry down and tuck them underneath to seal. (It's okay if it's not pretty; you'll slice this part off before serving.)

6 Place the Wellington in the freezer for 20 minutes. Remove it from the freezer, and flip it so the long side is parallel with the long side of the baking sheet. Brush the top of the puff pastry with more egg wash, and use a paring knife to score the top in a crosshatch pattern, being careful not to cut all the way through the pastry to the filling.

7 Bake for about 50 minutes, until the pastry is a deep, golden brown. Rotate the pan halfway through baking.

8 Make the gravy while the Wellington roasts: Heat the olive oil in a medium pot over medium heat. Whisk in the flour, and cook, stirring constantly, until the flour begins to darken and smells nutty, 1 to 2 minutes. Slowly drizzle in the vegetable stock while whisking constantly. Bring to a boil and then reduce to a low simmer. Whisk in the Dijon, add the thyme and bay leaf, and cook for about 5 minutes to thicken. For a thicker gravy, continue to cook to your desired consistency. Season with salt and pepper. Remove the bay leaf before serving.

9 To serve, slice the Wellington crosswise into slabs, and don't forget to pass the gravy.

VITAMIN C SALAD

Serves 8

Here, we harness the power of citrus for a bright, bold salad that's packed with enough vitamin C to keep scurvy at bay for several months, at least. The spicy arugula and aromatic herbs tie it all together. A mix of dill, mint, and parsley is definitely the way to go, but feel free to add a little basil if it suits you. To supreme the citrus, cut the tip off both ends of the fruit. Place it solidly on a cutting board, with one of the cut sides down for stabilization. Starting at the top and working your way down, cut off all of the peel, including the pith, revealing the fruit segments within. Slice between each membrane to free the segments. Supreming citrus is kind of a pain in the ass, to be honest, but it's exactly like flying first class: Once you do it, you'll never want to go back.

2 large grapefruits

2 large blood oranges

2 large mandarin oranges or tangerines

1 lemon

2 garlic cloves, minced

1½ tablespoons Dijon mustard

2 teaspoons honey

½ cup (120 ml) cup olive oil

Kosher salt and freshly ground black pepper

5 ounces (142 g) fresh arugula

4 celery ribs, sliced ⅛-inch-thick (3 mm) on a bias

½ cup (20 g) roughly chopped or torn fresh dill

½ cup (20 g) roughly chopped or torn fresh mint

½ cup (20 g) roughly chopped or torn fresh parsley

1 Supreme the grapefruits, blood oranges, mandarins, and lemon into a large bowl (see Headnote). Be sure to save the juices—that's what the bowl is for. Squeeze the spent membranes into the bowl and then use a slotted spoon to strain the segments from the juice and set them aside. Measure out ⅓ cup (80 ml) of the citrus juice, and store whatever is left over for another use—probably a mimosa.

2 Add the ⅓ cup (80 ml) of citrus juice back to the bowl, along with the garlic, Dijon, and honey. Whisk to combine. Slowly drizzle in the olive oil while constantly whisking, until the mixture is emulsified. Season with salt and pepper to taste.

3 Combine the arugula, celery, dill, mint, parsley, and citrus segments in a large salad bowl. Season with a little salt and pepper, and toss to combine. Add half of the dressing, and toss to combine. Add more dressing to taste, and serve immediately.

PREP AHEAD
Supreme the citrus and make the dressing up to 1 day in advance.

STEAKHOUSE CHOPPED SALAD

serves 8

Use all iceberg, all romaine, or a mix of both in this sort-of-classic steakhouse chopped salad. (By "steakhouse," we mean Sizzler; these are basically all the ingredients Courtney would choose from its salad bar.) Be sure to discard the outer leaves from the lettuces and wash them well before using. Salting the cukes ahead of time and patting them dry prevents their high liquid content from watering down the dressing. There is nothing worse than a salad with pale, watery tomatoes, so if you can't find good ones, keep them out. If tomatoes happen to be in season, though, chop some up and toss them in. If you have a mandoline, now would be a great time to use it.

1 English or 2 Persian cucumbers, peeled and sliced into ⅛-inch-thick (3 mm) coins

Kosher salt and freshly ground black pepper

¼ small red onion, sliced paper-thin (about ½ cup/115 g)

12 ounces (340 g) bacon, cut into ½-inch (1 cm) pieces

2 heads romaine or iceberg lettuce, roughly chopped (about 16 cups/570 g)

4 large button mushrooms, thinly shaved (about 1½ cups/100 g)

2 medium carrots, shredded (about 1 cup/90 g)

¼ cup (40 g) sunflower seeds, toasted

About 1 cup (230 g) Ramen Ranch Dressing (page 43)

4 ounces (113 g) blue cheese, crumbled (optional)

Garlic Toast Crunchies (page 37)

Frizzled Shallots (page 35)

1 Place the cucumber in a large bowl, and season with ¾ teaspoon salt. Set aside for 30 minutes to sweat.

2 Place the onion in a small bowl, cover it with ice water, and set it aside.

3 Meanwhile, cook the bacon in a large skillet over medium-low heat until crisp, 15 to 20 minutes. Use a slotted spoon to transfer the bacon to a paper towel–lined baking sheet. Save that bacon fat (see page 27)! Allow the bacon to cool to room temperature.

4 Combine the cooled bacon, lettuce, mushrooms, carrots, and sunflower seeds in a large salad bowl. Drain the onions and add them to the bowl. Use a paper towel to pat the cucumbers dry, and add them to the bowl as well. Season with salt and pepper, and give the salad a toss. Add a little over half of the Ramen Ranch Dressing, and toss again. Taste and add more dressing if desired.

5 Sprinkle generously with blue cheese (if using), Garlic Toast Crunchies, and Frizzled Shallots. Serve immediately with extra Garlic Toast Crunchies and Frizzled Shallots on the side.

SPECIAL EQUIPMENT
Mandoline

PREP AHEAD
Make the dressing, crunchies, and shallots up to 2 weeks in advance.

HACKABLE
Buy a couple of those premixed salad bags and toss in some bacon and any extra veggies you like.

PARTY PEOPLE HOUSE SALAD

Serves 8

If *Party People* were a brick-and-mortar establishment, this salad that would grace the menu every fall and winter. Like an old curmudgeon who never really learned how to love, radicchio becomes bitter as it ages. Don't let it push you away. Choose firm, crisp heads, and use them quickly. The sweetness from the apples and a little extra honey help combat bitterness, too. The most important ingredient, though, is the Fried Capers with their briny crunch. Use a mandoline on the apples for best results.

⅓ cup (80 ml) white wine vinegar

1 tablespoon plus 1 teaspoon Dijon mustard

1 tablespoon plus 1 teaspoon honey

¾ cup (180 ml) olive oil

Kosher salt and freshly ground black pepper

24 to 26 ounces (680 to 740 g) radicchio, outer leaves removed

1 large Honeycrisp or Pink Lady apple, cored and sliced into ⅛-inch-thick (3 mm) pieces

3 ounces (85 g) good-quality cheddar

½ cup (25 g) Fried Capers (page 36)

1 Combine the vinegar, Dijon, and honey in a small bowl. Vigorously whisk in the olive oil until it's emulsified. Season with salt (about ½ teaspoon) and pepper, and set aside.

2 Quarter and core the radicchio and then slice it into 1-inch (2.5 cm) strips. Add it to a large salad bowl along with the apple slices. Use a peeler to shave the cheddar on top, season with salt and black pepper, and toss to combine.

3 Pour in half of the dressing, toss to combine, and then add more dressing to taste.

4 Top with the Fried Capers, and serve within the hour.

SPECIAL EQUIPMENT
Mandoline

PREP AHEAD
Make the dressing up to 1 week in advance.

ALMOST CLASSIC CAESAR SALAD

Serves 8

A classic Caesar dressing contains Worcestershire sauce. We use Louisiana-style hot sauce instead, which is why, for legal reasons, we cannot call this a "classic Caesar salad." Ours does contain anchovies, though, but not too many. You'll taste them in an understated way. Add or subtract one or two to fit your palate, but don't skip them altogether: Even one will amp the flavor up significantly. Remove and discard the outer leaves of the romaine and wash it well before chopping. If you want to branch out, any crisp green like little gem, kale, or chicories would work well.

2 heads romaine, washed, dried, and torn into pieces (about 16 cups/570 g)

6 anchovy fillets in oil, drained

1 garlic clove

½ teaspoon kosher salt

2 ounces (55 g) Parmesan, finely grated (about ½ cup), plus more for serving

¼ cup (60 ml) fresh lemon juice

1 tablespoon Louisiana-style hot sauce

2 teaspoons Dijon mustard

1 egg yolk

¾ cup (180 ml) olive oil

Freshly ground black pepper

Garlic Toast Crunchies (page 37) or croutons of choice

1 Place the romaine in a large salad bowl, and set aside.

2 Add the anchovies, garlic, and salt to a mortar, and use a pestle to smash it into a paste. If you don't have a mortar and pestle, you can chop them together on a cutting board, using the flat side of your knife to smash and drag the mixture to help turn it into a paste.

3 Transfer the paste to a small bowl. Add the Parmesan, lemon juice, hot sauce, Dijon, and egg yolk, and whisk vigorously to combine. Slowly whisk in the olive oil until the dressing is thick and glossy.

4 Pour half of the dressing over the romaine spears. Add a few grinds of black pepper, and toss until the leaves are well coated. Add more dressing to taste, and season with more salt, if needed. Top with more Parmesan and a healthy dose of Garlic Toast Crunchies.

SPECIAL EQUIPMENT
Mortar and pestle

PREP AHEAD
Make the dressing up to 1 week in advance.

HACKABLE
Use your favorite store-bought Caesar dressing.

PASTA SALAD

Serves 8

Welcome to the early nineties, kids. If you weren't alive back then, or if you were too young to remember, this style of "salad" was in heavy rotation on the dinner menu circuit, usually made with fusilli pasta and a bottle of Newman's Own Italian dressing. While our hearts will always fondly remember that version, our brains have told us to update the recipe with orzo, homemade Giardiniera (page 32), and an Italian dressing that would make Paul Newman blush. Serve this salad chilled or at room temperature, and add some chopped, cured meat if you wanna.

1 English cucumber or 2 Persian cucumbers, halved lengthwise

Kosher salt

1½ cups (300 g) orzo

¾ cup (180 ml) olive oil

4½ tablespoons red wine vinegar

2 teaspoons Dijon mustard

2 garlic cloves, grated

Freshly ground black pepper

8 ounces (227 g) fresh mozzarella, drained and torn into bite-size pieces

1 cup (128 g) drained Giardiniera (page 32), roughly chopped

½ cup (75 g) pitted green olives, smashed and roughly chopped

1 large shallot, very thinly sliced

¼ cup (10 g) roughly chopped fresh Italian parsley (optional)

1 Place the cucumber halves flesh side down on a cutting board. Use a mallet or a rolling pin to gently smash them. Don't pulverize them; just give them little smacks until they start to fall apart. Break or slice them into bite-size chunks, transfer them to a small bowl, season with a healthy pinch of salt, and set aside.

2 Bring a pot of salted water to a boil over high heat. Add the orzo, and cook according to the package instructions to your desired softness.

3 While the orzo cooks, combine the olive oil, vinegar, Dijon, garlic, ½ teaspoon salt, and pepper in a large bowl, and whisk to emulsify.

4 Drain the orzo in a colander, and shake it a few times to get rid of any excess water. (Don't rinse it.) Immediately add the hot orzo to the dressing, mix to combine, and set it aside to cool to room temperature.

5 Drain the cucumbers and pat them dry. Add them along with the mozzarella, Giardiniera, olives, shallot, and parsley (if using) to the orzo bowl, and mix to combine.

6 Season with more salt and pepper if ya want. Serve immediately at room temperature, or store in the fridge for up to 4 days and serve chilled. She's great for picnics.

SPECIAL EQUIPMENT
Mallet or rolling pin

PREP AHEAD
Make the salad up to 4 days in advance.

HACKABLE
Use store-bought giardiniera.

THE SIMPLEST OF SALADS

serves 6 to 8

Everyone needs an embarrassingly easy, fast, and cheap salad recipe in their arsenal, and this is it. This isn't a *real* recipe, per se. You make the whole thing to taste. Use any kind of soft greens you like: Spinach, arugula, or butter lettuce are ideal. Two of those prewashed lettuce packages weigh 10 ounces (283 g), and that's how much you'll need. If you don't have lemons, use sherry or a red or white wine vinegar instead. And if you have any random veggies on deck, like carrots, scallions, radishes, or avocados, feel free to throw those in, too.

10 ounces (283 g) soft salad greens (like spinach, arugula, or butter lettuce)

3 tablespoons to ¼ cup (60 ml) olive oil

Kosher salt and freshly ground black pepper

2 to 4 teaspoons fresh lemon juice

Parmesan, for grating (optional)

Toasted nuts or seeds (optional)

1 Place the greens in a large salad bowl. Drizzle in enough olive oil to lightly coat the leaves. Toss, and season with salt and pepper.

2 Add some lemon juice to balance the flavor—make it as zingy as you like. Toss again.

3 Grate some Parmesan over the top, if you feel like it. Add some toasted nuts or seeds if you have any on hand. Serve immediately.

YOU SAY *TOMATO,* WE SAY *TONNATO*

Serves 8

Don't bother making this recipe if tomatoes aren't in season. If you do make this with sad tomatoes and don't think it tastes good, don't come for us, because then we'll be sad, too. And then you'll be sad that you made us sad. So it's best just to use the ripest, highest-quality tomatoes here. Use a serrated knife to cut them. Garlic Toast Crunchies (page 37) or Frizzled Shallots (page 35) would be great toppers for this, but the Fried Capers (page 36) are king.

2 pounds (907 g) heirloom or beefsteak tomatoes

Kosher or Maldon salt

1 cup (120 g) Tonnato (page 41)

Fried Capers (page 36)

1 Cut the tomatoes into ¼-inch-thick (6 mm) slices, and arrange them in an even layer on a large platter.

2 Season with salt, and spoon the Tonnato over the top.

3 Sprinkle generously with the Fried Capers, and serve.

PREP AHEAD
Make the Tonnato up to 3 days in advance.

CREAMED SPINACH

Serves 6 to 8

After blanching an inordinate amount of spinach, we cook it down, slow and low, for a rich and creamy consistency not unlike baby food, because baby food consistency is the reason why creamed spinach is so good. It should melt on your tongue. Be sure to use curly or adult flat leaf spinach, not baby spinach, which will fully disintegrate, and not in a good way. We want this to be like baby *food*, not baby poo.

3½ pounds (1.6 kg) adult spinach (5 to 6 bunches)

3 tablespoons unsalted butter

1 large shallot, finely chopped

Kosher salt and freshly ground black pepper

3 garlic cloves, thinly sliced

½ teaspoon red pepper flakes (optional)

2 tablespoons all-purpose flour

1½ cups (360 ml) heavy cream

1½ cups (360 ml) whole milk

Freshly grated nutmeg

Finely grated Parmesan (optional)

1 Bring 1 inch (2.5 cm) of water to boil in a large pot over medium-high heat. Add the spinach in batches, adding more on top as the spinach below wilts. Use tongs to move the wilted spinach to the top and push the raw spinach to the bottom. Cover the pot and cook until all the spinach has wilted, 3 to 5 minutes.

2 Drain the spinach, and rinse it under cold water. Squeeze out as much water as possible from the spinach and then roughly chop it and set it aside.

3 Heat the butter in a large pot over medium-low heat. Add the shallot, season with salt and pepper, and cook until soft, about 4 minutes. Add the garlic and red pepper flakes (if using), and cook for 30 seconds. Add the flour, and cook, stirring constantly, until the flour starts to smell a little nutty, about 1 more minute.

4 Slowly add the heavy cream and milk while whisking constantly. Increase the heat to medium-high, and bring the mixture to a simmer while stirring.

5 Reduce the heat to low, and add the spinach. Season with salt, pepper, and several grates of nutmeg. Continue to cook on low, stirring occasionally, until the spinach is very soft and the sauce thickens, about 30 minutes. You'll need to stir it more often toward the end of cooking to prevent the bottom from burning. Season with more salt, pepper, and nutmeg if needed.

6 If you're feeling fancy, transfer the creamed spinach to a 1-quart (1 L) baking dish, top with some finely grated Parmesan (if using), and throw that sucker under the broiler for about 2 minutes to brown the cheese.

PREP AHEAD

Make the creamed spinach through step 5 up to 4 days in advance. Reheat it on the stovetop over medium heat, thinning it out with a little water if needed, and continue on with step 6 if desired.

LEMONY MISO BUTTER BEANS

Serves 6 to 8

Butter beans and lima beans are the exact same thing, and if you don't like them, cannellini beans are a great substitution. Whatever you use, make sure to buy fresh dried beans; old ones that have been sitting in the back of your pantry for years will never fully soften. When you soak the beans, the ones that float to the top are stale, so toss them out. Adding a Parmesan rind to the cooking liquid gives the beans a nutty flavor. If that sounds good to you, throw one in there. Once the beans are cooked, we bathe them in a generous amount of creamy, salty Miso Butter (page 42). The finished product is fantastic slathered on a hunky piece of crusty bread next to any of our Showstopping Mains (pages 146 to 154).

1 pound (454 g) dried butter beans, soaked in water overnight and drained

2 fresh rosemary or thyme sprigs

1 Parmesan rind (optional)

Kosher salt

3 tablespoons Miso Butter (page 42), plus more for serving

4 garlic cloves, thinly sliced

½ teaspoon red pepper flakes (optional)

1 cup (240 ml) chicken or vegetable stock, or water

¼ cup (27 g) finely grated Parmesan, plus more for serving

Juice of ½ lemon

1 Add the beans to a large pot, and cover with water by 2 inches (5 cm). Add the rosemary or thyme (or both, if you're feeling yourself). If you have a Parmesan rind handy, throw that in there, too (but only if you're *really* feeling yourself). Season the water with salt, set over medium-high heat, and bring to a boil. Reduce the heat to low, cover, and cook until the beans are soft, about 90 minutes. Drain the beans, remove the herb stems and Parmesan rind, if you used one, and set aside.

2 Wipe the pot out if needed. Add the Miso Butter to the now-empty pot, and set over medium-high heat. Add the garlic and red pepper flakes (if using), and sizzle until fragrant, about 30 seconds.

3 Add the beans, and stir to coat. Use a potato masher or a wooden spoon to smash about one-third of the beans. (No need to be super specific here.)

4 Add the stock or water, bring to a simmer, and cook for 1 to 2 minutes to thicken. Keep in mind that the beans will thicken more as they cool. Remove from the heat, and stir in the Parmesan and lemon juice.

5 Add the beans to a serving bowl, and top with a pat of Miso Butter and more Parmesan.

PREP AHEAD
Make the beans up to 4 days in advance. Reheat on the stove over medium heat. Add a little bit of water to thin them out if needed.

HACKABLE
Use four 15-ounce (425 g) cans of cannellini beans, drained and rinsed, and start with step 2.

BLISTERED BROCCOLI
with Chiles and Cashews

Serves 8

This quick-and-easy vegan recipe is great as is, but if you want to kick it up a notch, shower it with some Sichuan chili crisp at the end. Use raw cashews; they will roast along with the broccoli. If you can only find roasted cashews, wait until step 4 to use them, and add them along with the garlic.

2 pounds (907 g) broccoli, cut into 2-inch-long (5 cm) florets

⅓ cup (50 g) roughly chopped raw cashews

½ teaspoon red pepper flakes (optional)

Kosher salt

6 tablespoons olive oil, divided

4 garlic cloves, minced

Juice of ½ lemon

Sichuan chili crisp (optional)

1 Preheat the oven to 425°F (215°C).

2 Divide the broccoli, cashews, and red pepper flakes (if using) between two large, rimmed baking sheets. Season the broccoli on each baking sheet with salt and then toss each with 3 tablespoons olive oil until well coated.

3 Roast the broccoli for about 15 minutes, without stirring, until it's very browned and blistered in some spots.

4 Combine all the broccoli onto one of the baking sheets, and toss it with the garlic. Bake for 3 more minutes, until the garlic is fragrant and the broccoli has softened but still retains some bite.

5 Spritz the broccoli with some lemon juice and drizzle with chili crisp (if using).

COCONUT LIME RICE PILAF

Serves 8

Makrut lime leaves, garlic, ginger, and coconut milk bring the flavor to this easy baked rice dish. Makrut lime leaves can be found in Asian grocery stores or online. If you have trouble sourcing them, you can substitute with the peel of one large lime. Leftovers make excellent fried rice (just saying).

2 cups (400 g) long-grain white rice (basmati or jasmine)

3 tablespoons unsalted butter

1 yellow onion, thinly sliced

4 Makrut lime leaves

3 garlic cloves, thinly sliced

2 teaspoons freshly grated ginger

½ teaspoon ground turmeric

One 13.5-ounce (400 ml) can full-fat coconut milk

2 tablespoons sugar

1 teaspoon kosher salt

2 tablespoons chopped fresh cilantro

1 lime, sliced into wedges

1 Rinse the rice in a large sieve until the water runs clear. Put the rice in a container, and cover it with water. Let it soak for 1 hour and then drain.

2 Preheat the oven to 425°F (215°C).

3 Heat the butter in a large Dutch oven over medium heat until it melts and starts to bubble. Add the onion, and cook until translucent, about 4 minutes. Add the lime leaves, garlic, ginger, and turmeric, and cook until fragrant, about 1 minute. Stir in the rice and continue to cook, scraping up the bottom of the pan, until the rice is evenly coated and begins to sizzle, about 1 more minute. Remove from the heat.

4 Meanwhile, add the coconut milk, sugar, and salt to a medium pot. Fill the empty coconut milk can with water and pour that into the pot. Repeat one more time so you have 2 cans-worth of water in the pot. Set over medium-high heat, and bring to a boil. Immediately pour the mixture over the rice.

5 Cover the rice tightly, and bake for about 30 minutes, until all of the liquid has been absorbed and the rice starts to crisp around the edges.

6 Remove from the oven, and let the dish rest, covered, for 10 minutes. Fluff the rice, season with more salt if desired, top with the cilantro, and serve with the lime wedges on the side.

TWICE-BAKED POTATOES

Serves 8

Twice-baked potatoes are Brie's grandma's signature side dish. She says you *have* to mix the filling while the potatoes are still hot to prevent gumminess. And she's right. Doing it this way makes it easier to incorporate the ingredients without overmixing the potatoes, which will cause them to release more of their gluey starch. Use a potato ricer in step 6 for added protection. By the way, this recipe is a blank slate for your own fever-dream version of twice-baked potatoes. Add some bacon if you want to. Throw in a few scallions; we won't complain. We once heard a tale of a woman who put hot dogs in hers. The moral of this story is to dream big.

2 tablespoons olive oil

½ teaspoon kosher salt

8 russet potatoes, 7 to 8 ounces (198 to 227 g) each, washed, dried, and pierced with a fork

½ cup (120 ml) whole milk

1 stick (8 tablespoons) unsalted butter

½ cup (110 g) sour cream

Freshly ground black pepper

4 ounces (113 g) Colby-Jack, shredded (about 1 cup)

Sweet or hot paprika

Finely chopped fresh chives

1 Preheat the oven to 400°F (200°C).

2 Mix the olive oil and salt in a medium bowl. Add the potatoes to the bowl, one or two at a time, and toss to coat with the salty oil. Place the potatoes on a large, rimmed baking sheet.

3 Transfer the potatoes directly to the upper rack of the oven, and place the baking sheet on the rack below them to catch any drips. Bake for 60 to 75 minutes, until the potatoes are cooked through. (You'll be able to easily pierce them with a paring knife.) Remove them from the oven, and let them cool for about 10 minutes. They will still be quite hot. Leave the oven on if you are planning to bake the potatoes right away.

4 While the potatoes cool, heat the milk and butter in a small pot over medium heat. Don't let it boil; just melt the butter and warm the milk.

5 Hold the potatoes with tongs or a kitchen towel to protect your hands from the heat, and cut them in half lengthwise. Scoop the flesh into a large bowl, leaving a ¼-inch (6 mm) border of potato on the insides of the skin. Place the scooped-out halves on the baking sheet.

6 Mash the potato filling with a masher or fork, or run it through a ricer. Add the hot milk mixture and the sour cream, and mix to combine. Season with salt and pepper (don't be shy!) and then fold in the Colby-Jack.

7 Season the insides of the hollowed-out potatoes with a little salt and pepper and then use a spoon or a small ice cream scoop to portion the filling back into the potato halves, 2 to 3 tablespoons per half. Top each with a sprinkle of paprika and some chives.

8 Bake the potatoes right away, for about 10 minutes, until the cheese has melted and the tops have lightly browned.

PREP AHEAD
Make the potatoes through step 7 and refrigerate for up to 4 days or freeze for up to 1 month. If refrigerating, bake from chilled according to step 8, add a few more minutes of bake time as needed. Bake from frozen for about 30 minutes, until the potatoes are heated through and the tops have lightly browned.

FREEZABLE

SAVORY DROP BISCUITS

Serves 6 to 8

We drew inspiration for this recipe from Red Lobster's Cheddar Bay Biscuits, one of the greatest biscuit recipes to ever exist. Brushed with a savory garlic butter right after they come out of the oven, a basket full of these babies would be a welcome sight on any dinner table. They will also make your kitchen smell divine.

1¾ cups (245 g) all-purpose flour

2¼ teaspoons baking powder

2 teaspoons dried minced onion

1½ teaspoons sugar

1 teaspoon garlic powder

¾ teaspoon kosher salt

½ teaspoon baking soda

1 stick (8 tablespoons) cold, unsalted butter, cut into ½-inch (1 cm) cubes

3 ounces (85 g) shredded Gruyère (about 1 cup)

1 cup (240 ml) buttermilk

3 tablespoons unsalted butter

1 garlic clove, minced

2 tablespoons chopped fresh parsley

1 egg, beaten with 1 teaspoon water

Maldon salt

1 Whisk together the flour, baking powder, minced onion, sugar, garlic powder, kosher salt, and baking soda in large bowl.

2 Add the cold cubed butter to the bowl, and toss the butter with the flour mixture to coat it. Use your hands to cut the butter into the flour until it is pea-sized and mealy, with no big chunks of butter remaining. (You could also do this in a food processor, but where's the fun in that?). Add the Gruyère, and toss to evenly combine. Place the bowl in the freezer for 30 minutes.

3 Remove the bowl from the freezer, add the buttermilk, and mix until a shaggy dough forms. Cover the bowl, and refrigerate the dough for 30 minutes to hydrate it.

4 While the biscuit dough rests, add the butter and garlic to a small pan and set over low heat to melt the butter. Continue heating to infuse the butter with the garlic, 1 to 2 more minutes, being careful not to let the garlic brown. Remove from the heat, and stir in the parsley.

5 Preheat the oven to 425°F (215°C). Line a large baking sheet with parchment paper.

6 Use a spoon or a 2-ounce (¼ cup/60 ml) scoop to drop 12 mounds of the biscuit dough onto the baking sheet. Make sure they are evenly spaced, but it's okay if they are kind of close to one another. Place the baking sheet in the freezer for 5 minutes.

7 Remove the baking sheet from the freezer, brush the tops with the egg wash, and sprinkle the tops with Maldon salt. Bake the biscuits for about 25 minutes, until golden brown. Remove from the oven, brush the garlic parsley butter over the tops, and serve.

PREP AHEAD

Make, scoop, and store the biscuit dough in the freezer, well wrapped, up to 1 month in advance. Bake from frozen according to step 7. You may need to add a few minutes of bake time. Make the garlic butter up to 2 weeks in advance. Store in the fridge and melt just before using.

FREEZABLE

fancy party plans

Congratulations! You did a really hard thing that you thought you couldn't pull off, but you totally pulled it off!

menu

Old Pal (page 52), Slow-Roasted Olives (page 68), A Roast Beef for Us All (page 149), Almost Classic Caesar Salad (page 162), Creamed Spinach (page 170), Twice-Baked Potatoes (page 178), Brown Butter Pecan Blondies (page 102), a selection of digestifs, coffee, or tea (optional).

ambiance & dress

Check out page 145 for tips on ambiance and dress.

Well, friend, YOU DID IT AGAIN! That thing you thought you could not do, you went ahead and crushed it anyway. You are strong. You are brave. You are wise. It's time to bask in the glow of soft candlelight, creamed spinach, and pride. Take a few pats on the back along with those twice-baked potatoes. It's not every day we go to bat for ourselves and hit one out of the park. Better collect your trophy (your trophy, of course, being a glorious night to remember—or possibly forget, depending on how many Old Pals you drink).

prep plan

two days out: Make the salad dressing and the Garlic Toast Crunchies (if using); make the Old Pal base; make the olives; salt the roast beef; make any of the accompanying sauces.

one day out: Set up decorations (if using); stage serving utensils, platters, plates, and napkins; set up as much of the bar area as possible; make the spinach through step 5; make the potatoes through step 7; make the roast beef through step 3.

morning of the party: Make the blondies.

as guests arrive: Set out the Old Pal, drink garnishes, and ice in the bar area; warm the olives, if desired, and serve.

just before dinner: Finish the roast beef; toss the salad; reheat the spinach and continue on with step 6, if desired; bake the potatoes and serve.

after dinner: Slice and serve the blondies with a digestif, coffee, or tea, if desired.

playlist suggestions

Include songs about achieving success through hard work and tenacity. Things like "Eye of the Tiger" by Survivor, "We Are the Champions" by Queen, "Don't Stop Believin'" by Journey, and "Nothing's Gonna Stop Us Now" by Starship.

the brag and complain

This is a time-honored tradition from circa 2015, when Brie held the first official Brag and Complain symposium. Our culture typically shuns those who brag and/or complain, but not tonight! Tonight, everyone gets a chance to tell it like it is. And it is amazing. Either during or after dinner, simply open up the table to anyone who has something they'd like to brag or complain about. From there, all a participant needs to do is say "I have something to [brag/complain] about!" Then everyone listens intently, chiming in as needed, as they do just that. It might be slow going at first, but after a few turns, you'll be surprised at how quickly those floodgates open.

menu

Scorpion Slush (page 61), Piña Colada JELL-O Shots (page 65), California "Hand Rolls" (page 83), Kalua Pork (page 150), Vitamin C Salad (page 157), Coconut Lime Rice Pilaf (page 177), Pineapple Right-Side-Up Cake (page 94), a selection of digestifs, coffee, or tea (optional).

playlist suggestions

Think upscale steakhouse or Buckingham Palace. The Brandenburg Concertos by Johann Sebastian Bach, the soundtrack to *Amadeus*, or really to any of your favorite blockbuster films, especially if they are scored by John Williams, Hans Zimmer, or Ennio Morricone.

Check out page 145 for tips on ambiance and dress.

prep plan

two days out: Make the scorpion base through step 1 or, if blending, through step 4; make the pineapple cake through step 12.

one day out: Set up decorations (if using); stage serving utensils, platters, plates, and napkins; set up as much of the bar area as possible; make the pork; make the salad through step 2; finish the cake; make the piña colada shots through step 4.

morning of the party: Make step 1 of the hand rolls; prepare the mise en place for the coconut rice; finish the piña colada shots.

as guests arrive: Pull out the cake to bring to room temperature; slush the scorpion base and serve; serve the shots; finish and serve the hand rolls; bake the coconut rice.

just before dinner: Reheat the pork; finish the salad; serve both with the coconut rice.

after dinner: Slice and serve the cake with a digestif, coffee, or tea, if desired.

the happiest of birthdays

Another year around the sun, another fancy dinner party to throw. We based this menu solely on what Courtney would want if it were her birthday, and we think you'll love it, too. Plus, that Texas sheet cake looks real pretty ablaze with candles (see page 92).

menu

Tex-Mex Martini (page 52), Party People Peño Poppers (PPPP; page 84), Salsa Verde Snapper (page 153), Steakhouse Chopped Salad (page 158), Lemony Miso Butter Beans (page 173), Courtney's Grandma's Texas Sheet Cake (page 97), a selection of digestifs, coffee, or tea (optional).

playlist suggestions

Ask the birthday person what their favorite songs are and be sure to include all of them. Other than that, anything goes.

Check out page 145 for tips on ambiance and dress.

prep plan

two days out: Make the martini base and the Chile Lime Salt (for the snapper and the martinis); make the Ramen Ranch Dressing, Garlic Toast Crunchies, and Frizzled Shallots (for the salad).

one day out: Set up decorations (if using); stage serving utensils, platters, plates, and napkins; set up as much of the bar area as possible; make the peño poppers through step 4; make the salsa verde for the snapper; make the Pico de Gallo and Lime Crème Fraîche for the snapper (if using); make the Miso Butter and soak the butter beans.

morning of the party: Make the cake; prep the mise en place for the salad; make the miso butter beans through step 4.

as guests arrive: Set the martini, drink garnishes, and ice out in the bar area; bake and serve the poppers.

just before dinner: Toss the salad; roast the snapper and heat the tortillas; reheat the butter beans and serve.

after dinner: Slice and serve the cake with a digestif, coffee, or tea, if desired.

tiny parties

Tiny parties are so stinking cute and the perfect size if you happen to be a Shy One (see page 16). They include date nights, silly hangs with your BFF, and even couch-potato parties of one—you are the only person who's *always* guaranteed to be around, so why not show yourself a good time? Just because the head count is low doesn't mean you can't eat well. This chapter is divided into three sections: tiny mains, tiny sides, and tiny desserts. Choose one recipe from each section, and add a bottle of wine, some beers, or your favorite soft beverage. You can omit the Party Essentials section for this romp.

SKIP'S PEACH CHICKEN

serves 2 to 3

This dish was a staple at Brie's house growing up. Her family typically eats it over a mound of savory cornbread stuffing, but a pan of freshly baked cornbread, rice, or a crusty loaf of sourdough would also fit the bill. The original recipe uses boneless chicken thighs. We've opted for whole, bone-in chicken legs here. The chicken is braised in the oven along with the peaches and their juice, making this dish feel like a mash-up of French coq au vin blanc (subbing peach juice for wine) and Chinese American orange chicken. The thighs and drumsticks can be attached or separated, or feel free to use all thighs or all drumsticks. Canned peaches come packed in heavy syrup, light syrup, or just juice. You can use any of these options. The cloves add a lovely earthy note, but feel free to play around with other spices if you like. Hot, sweet, or even smoked paprika, allspice, or ginger would all be great.

4 whole chicken legs

Kosher salt and freshly ground black pepper

2 tablespoons olive oil

One 15-ounce (425 g) can peach slices, with juice

¼ teaspoon ground cloves

2 tablespoons roughly chopped fresh parsley

1 Preheat the oven to 325°F (165°C).

2 Pat the chicken dry, and season it on both sides with salt and pepper.

3 Heat the olive oil in a large, ovenproof skillet or Dutch oven over medium-high heat until it shimmers. Add the chicken legs, and cook on one side until deeply browned, about 4 minutes. Flip over the chicken, and cook on the other side until deeply browned, another 3 to 4 minutes.

4 Reduce the heat to low. Pour the peaches and the juice from the can into the skillet, and stir in the cloves. Bring the mixture to a simmer, and transfer it to the oven. Bake for 1 hour, until the chicken is tender and a knife easily cuts through it.

5 Transfer the chicken to a platter, put the pan back on the stovetop, and bring the peaches and the juice to a boil over high heat. Continue cooking until the peaches break down and the sauce reduces to a glaze-like consistency, about 3 minutes. Season with salt, spoon the peach glaze over the chicken, and sprinkle with parsley to serve.

PREP AHEAD
The chicken can be made up to 3 days in advance, stored in the fridge, and reheated, covered, in a 325°F (165°C) oven.

FAJITAS FOR TWO

serves 4 . . . jk, serves 2

We prefer to use skirt steak for fajitas due to its higher fat content, but you can use flank or flap. Sometimes skirt and flap are really thin; if that's the case with yours, fold it in half to double its thickness before searing. This will allow the meat to brown without the risk of overcooking it. Flank, on the other hand, is usually a thicker cut, so it may take a couple extra minutes to get it to the right temp. For best results, cook the steak to medium rare or just a hair shy of medium. You can use a poblano, Hatch, bell, or Anaheim pepper for the large green chile. Purists don't usually eat fajitas with cheese. We are not purists. Serve these alongside a bowl of Delicious Beans!!! (page 199), and you won't regret it.

1½ tablespoons fresh lime juice

1½ tablespoons grapeseed, canola, or vegetable oil

¾ teaspoon chili powder

½ teaspoon ground cumin

¾ teaspoon kosher salt, plus more for seasoning

3 garlic cloves, roughly chopped

¾ pound (340 g) skirt steak

Six 6-inch (15 cm) flour tortillas

2 tablespoons canola or grapeseed oil, divided

1 large green chile, seeded and sliced into ¼-inch-thick (6 mm) strips

1 large jalapeño, seeded and sliced into ¼-inch-thick (6 mm) strips

½ yellow onion, sliced with the grain into ¼-inch-thick (6 mm) strips

FOR SERVING

Guacamole

Lime Crème Fraîche (page 41) or sour cream

Pico de Gallo (page 33) or salsa

Shredded Colby-Jack (optional)

1 Combine the lime juice, oil, chili powder, cumin, salt, and garlic in a small bowl.

2 Place the steak in a large zipper-top bag, and pour the marinade over the steak. Seal the bag so it still contains some air, and shake it to coat the steak. Open the bag, reseal it to get as much air out of it as possible, and squish the steak around a few times. Refrigerate for at least 8 hours or, even better, 24. Squish the bag every few hours to make sure the marinade is evenly distributed.

3 Preheat the oven to 300°F (150°C).

4 Stack the tortillas: Wet your fingers and flick a little bit of water on top of each tortilla before stacking another on top of it. Wrap the tortillas in foil, and set them in the oven to warm for about 10 minutes.

5 Remove the steak from the marinade, pat dry, and season with a little more salt.

6 Heat 1 tablespoon oil in a large skillet or cast-iron pan over high heat until it begins to shimmer. Working in batches, sear a piece of steak on one side until deeply browned, 2 to 3 minutes. Flip over the steak and cook on the other side until browned, about 1 minute more. Transfer to a cutting board, and repeat with the remaining steak. Allow the seared steak to rest for 15 minutes.

7 Meanwhile, cook the veggies. Add the remaining oil to the skillet, and set over high heat. Add the chile, jalapeño, and onion, and cook, without stirring, until the veggies are lightly charred on the edges, about 2 minutes. Season with salt, and cook, stirring occasionally, until soft, about 5 minutes. Remove from the heat.

8 Slice the steak against the grain into strips. Return the steak and all of its juices to the pan, and mix with the vegetables. Heat on high for 30 seconds to meld the flavors.

9 Serve with the tortillas, guacamole, Lime Crème Fraîche, Pico de Gallo, and Colby-Jack (if using).

PREP AHEAD

Marinate the steak 1 day in advance. Store in an airtight container in the fridge.

HACKABLE

Use store-bought guacamole, salsa, and sour cream.

FETTUCCINE RANCHO ALFREDO

serves 2

We put a recipe for A Different Tuna Helper (page 129) in this book, which you should definitely make because it is delicious, but if you want something that tastes more like the original, boxed version of Tuna Helper that we all know and love, this recipe is the way to go. It's fantastic plain, but it welcomes the addition of shrimp, chunks of chicken, or, yes, even a can of tuna (see Note). A wilted mound of baby kale or spinach is a tasty (and healthy!) and completely optional touch. Instead of draining the pasta, we transfer it directly to the pan, bringing sloshes of the cooking water with it to help wilt the greens (if using) and emulsify the Parmesan. For a lighter version, feel free to substitute half-and-half for the heavy cream.

1 tablespoon unsalted butter

1 large garlic clove, thinly sliced

¾ cup (180 ml) heavy cream

1 tablespoon Ramen Ranch Seasoning (page 43)

½ pound (227 g) fettuccine

5 ounces (142 g) baby kale or spinach (optional)

2 ounces (55 g) Parmesan, finely grated (about ½ cup), plus more for serving

Kosher salt and freshly ground black pepper

1 Bring a large pot of heavily salted water to a boil over high heat.

2 Meanwhile, heat the butter in a large, deep skillet over medium heat until foamy. Add the garlic, and cook for 30 seconds. Add the heavy cream and Ramen Ranch Seasoning, and whisk to combine. Bring to a simmer and then cover and turn off the heat.

3 Add the fettuccine to the pot of boiling water, and cook according to the package instructions until al dente.

4 Use tongs or a spider to transfer the pasta directly to the skillet. Toss the pasta to coat over low heat.

5 Add the greens (if using), and toss until wilted.

6 Add the Parmesan in three batches, allowing it to fully incorporate before adding more, and continue to toss until the sauce thickens. Season with salt (or, even better, more Ramen Ranch Seasoning) and pepper to taste, and add more pasta water to thin the sauce if desired.

7 Divide the mixture among serving bowls, top with more Parmesan, and serve immediately.

NOTE
Brown any meaty additions over high heat in step 2. Remove it from the pan before lowering the heat to medium and adding the garlic. Toss the meat back into the pasta in step 6 before adding the Parmesan.

SPECIAL EQUIPMENT
Tongs or a spider

FAJITAS FOR TWO

serves 4 . . . jk, serves 2

We prefer to use skirt steak for fajitas due to its higher fat content, but you can use flank or flap. Sometimes skirt and flap are really thin; if that's the case with yours, fold it in half to double its thickness before searing. This will allow the meat to brown without the risk of overcooking it. Flank, on the other hand, is usually a thicker cut, so it may take a couple extra minutes to get it to the right temp. For best results, cook the steak to medium rare or just a hair shy of medium. You can use a poblano, Hatch, bell, or Anaheim pepper for the large green chile. Purists don't usually eat fajitas with cheese. We are not purists. Serve these alongside a bowl of Delicious Beans!!! (page 199), and you won't regret it.

1½ tablespoons fresh lime juice

1½ tablespoons grapeseed, canola, or vegetable oil

¾ teaspoon chili powder

½ teaspoon ground cumin

¾ teaspoon kosher salt, plus more for seasoning

3 garlic cloves, roughly chopped

¾ pound (340 g) skirt steak

Six 6-inch (15 cm) flour tortillas

2 tablespoons canola or grapeseed oil, divided

1 large green chile, seeded and sliced into ¼-inch-thick (6 mm) strips

1 large jalapeño, seeded and sliced into ¼-inch-thick (6 mm) strips

½ yellow onion, sliced with the grain into ¼-inch-thick (6 mm) strips

FOR SERVING

Guacamole

Lime Crème Fraîche (page 41) or sour cream

Pico de Gallo (page 33) or salsa

Shredded Colby-Jack (optional)

1   Combine the lime juice, oil, chili powder, cumin, salt, and garlic in a small bowl.

2   Place the steak in a large zipper-top bag, and pour the marinade over the steak. Seal the bag so it still contains some air, and shake it to coat the steak. Open the bag, reseal it to get as much air out of it as possible, and squish the steak around a few times. Refrigerate for at least 8 hours or, even better, 24. Squish the bag every few hours to make sure the marinade is evenly distributed.

3   Preheat the oven to 300°F (150°C).

4   Stack the tortillas: Wet your fingers and flick a little bit of water on top of each tortilla before stacking another on top of it. Wrap the tortillas in foil, and set them in the oven to warm for about 10 minutes.

5   Remove the steak from the marinade, pat dry, and season with a little more salt.

6   Heat 1 tablespoon oil in a large skillet or cast-iron pan over high heat until it begins to shimmer. Working in batches, sear a piece of steak on one side until deeply browned, 2 to 3 minutes. Flip over the steak and cook on the other side until browned, about 1 minute more. Transfer to a cutting board, and repeat with the remaining steak. Allow the seared steak to rest for 15 minutes.

7   Meanwhile, cook the veggies. Add the remaining oil to the skillet, and set over high heat. Add the chile, jalapeño, and onion, and cook, without stirring, until the veggies are lightly charred on the edges, about 2 minutes. Season with salt, and cook, stirring occasionally, until soft, about 5 minutes. Remove from the heat.

8   Slice the steak against the grain into strips. Return the steak and all of its juices to the pan, and mix with the vegetables. Heat on high for 30 seconds to meld the flavors.

9   Serve with the tortillas, guacamole, Lime Crème Fraîche, Pico de Gallo, and Colby-Jack (if using).

PREP AHEAD
Marinate the steak 1 day in advance. Store in an airtight container in the fridge.

HACKABLE
Use store-bought guacamole, salsa, and sour cream.

LOW-BAKED SALMON
in Miso Butter
serves 2 to 3

We originally titled this recipe "Slow-Baked Salmon in Miso Butter," but our recipe tester, Bee, pointed out that it's not really that slow of a bake if it's over and done with in 20 minutes. This gave us pause. What other things in life do we call "slow" that are actually fast? Have we ever noticed the sands of time at all, or do we just ignore it as it falls through our outstretched fingertips? What is life anyway, if not a slow-bake? In our defense, it does take a teensy bit longer to cook the salmon due to the oven's extremely low temperature. This prevents overcooking, making the salmon extra succulent and moist. The togarashi adds a nutty, piquant, citrusy depth to the dish. Don't skip it. If you don't have an ovenproof skillet, use whatever you do have for the stovetop and transfer the salmon to a small baking dish before you put it in the oven.

½ cup (116 g) Miso Butter (page 42)
1 teaspoon shichimi togarashi
1 pound (454 g) skinless salmon fillet
Kosher salt
1 scallion, thinly sliced

FOR SERVING
Cucumber slices
Lemon wedges

1 Preheat the oven to 300°F (150°C).

2 Place the Miso Butter and togarashi in an ovenproof skillet that's large enough to hold the salmon. Set over medium-low heat, and cook, stirring occasionally, until the butter is bubbling and fragrant, about 3 minutes. Remove from the heat.

3 Pat the salmon dry, season with salt on both sides, and add it to the skillet. Flip it around once to give it a bath in the butter mixture. Transfer the pan to the oven, and roast the salmon, uncovered, for 15 to 20 minutes, until it just turns opaque and flakes easily, basting once halfway through cooking.

4 Break the salmon into large chunks, and transfer it to a serving platter. Drizzle with some of the Miso Butter, and top with the scallions. Serve with sliced cucumber and lemon wedges on the side.

CHILLED TOFU
with Sesame Spinach
serves 2

The star ingredient in this recipe is the chili crisp: a spicy Sichuan condiment that magically transforms everything it touches into a mouth-tingling paradise. Courtney once said she'd eat a shoe if it were dunked in the stuff. Hopefully we'll never need to test her on this. Pressing the tofu releases a ton of water and makes room for it to soak up all the other salty, yummy, umami flavors. Use two large cans of tomato sauce, a 5-pound (2.3 kg) bag of flour, several cookbooks, or an actual weight to press the tofu. The finished dish is great on its own, or it can be served over freshly steamed rice for a full meal. Just don't forget that final drizzle of the star ingredient at the end.

One 14-ounce (397 g) block firm tofu

¼ cup (60 ml) soy sauce

1 teaspoon chili crisp, plus more for serving

1 tablespoon grapeseed or canola oil

¼ teaspoon sesame oil

1 garlic clove, thinly sliced

10 ounces (283 g) fresh spinach

Kosher salt

FOR SERVING
Toasted sesame seeds
Frizzled Shallots (page 35)
Sliced scallions

1 Cut the tofu in half lengthwise into two blocks. Line a rimmed baking sheet with a clean dish towel, and place the tofu on top of the towel. Cover the tofu with another clean dish towel, and place another baking sheet or baking dish on top. Place about 4 pounds (1.8 kg) of weight on top of the pan, and press the tofu for 20 to 30 minutes. Replace the dish towel on top with a new one halfway through.

2 Cut the pressed tofu into 1-inch (2.5 cm) cubes, and transfer them to a medium container with an airtight lid. Pour the soy sauce and chili crisp on top. Put on the lid, and invert the container a few times to make sure all the tofu is coated in the sauce. Store in the fridge for at least 2 hours, flipping the container every 30 minutes to evenly coat the tofu.

3 Heat the grapeseed oil and sesame oil in a large skillet over medium-low heat. Add the garlic, and cook for 30 seconds. Don't let it brown.

4 Add as much spinach as will fit in the pan, season with a little salt, and cook until just wilted, adding more spinach when there's space, about 2 minutes. Season with more salt to taste, keeping in mind that we are serving this with the tofu, which will already be quite salty. Remove from the heat, and allow the spinach to cool to room temperature.

5 Drain and squeeze the spinach gently to remove any excess water and then toss it with the marinated tofu. Serve immediately, or chill overnight. It can be eaten chilled or at room temperature. Drizzle with more chili crisp, and generously top with toasted sesame seeds, Frizzled Shallots, and/or sliced scallions to serve.

PREP AHEAD
Make the tofu up to 2 days in advance.

DELICIOUS BEANS!!!

serves 2 to 3

This is a hybrid of Cajun-style red beans and Tex-Mex-style refried beans. The bacon adds a distinct porky smokiness. It can be omitted if you are a vegetarian, but otherwise, don't even think about it. The serrano bumps up the spice quotient, so if you are adverse, use a small jalapeño instead (they are typically less spicy) or omit the pepper altogether. Make sure to buy fresh dried beans; the old ones that have been sitting in the back of your pantry for years will never fully soften. When you soak the beans, the ones that float to the top are stale, so toss them out.

1 to 2 tablespoons unsalted butter

2 strips bacon, thinly sliced (optional)

½ yellow onion, roughly chopped

1 serrano pepper, roughly chopped

Kosher salt

½ pound (227 g) dried red, black, or pinto beans (about 1 cup), soaked in water overnight and drained

1 bay leaf

FOR SERVING (OPTIONAL)

Cooked rice

1 scallion, thinly sliced

Hot sauce

1 Add 1 tablespoon butter and the bacon (if using) to a large pot, and set over medium heat. (If you aren't using bacon, add 2 tablespoons butter to the pot.) When the bacon (or just the butter) starts to sizzle, add the onion and serrano, season with salt, and cook until the onions are translucent, about 5 minutes.

2 Add the beans and bay leaf, and cover with water by 1 inch (2.5 cm). Season with more salt, and bring to a boil. Reduce the heat to low, cover, and cook until the beans are very soft, about 90 minutes.

3 Remove the bay leaf from the pot, and use a spider or a large, slotted spoon to transfer the beans to a food processor or blender. Add ½ cup (120 ml) of the cooking liquid, and pulse a few times to your desired consistency. (We like ours a little chunky.) Add more cooking liquid to thin the beans if you like. They'll thicken quite a bit as they cool.

4 Season with more salt. Serve over rice, topped with scallions and some hot sauce (if using), or as a stand-alone side.

SPECIAL EQUIPMENT

Spider, food processor or blender

PREP AHEAD

Make these beans through step 3 up to 4 days in advance. Store in an airtight container in the fridge. Reheat over medium-low heat, thinning with more water, as needed.

HACKABLE

Use two 15-ounce (425 g) cans of beans, drained and rinsed. Add about 1 cup (240 ml) water (instead of covering them by 1 inch/2.5 cm), and reduce the cooking time to 15 minutes.

FUN DIP FRIES

serves 2

Remember how much fun Fun Dip was? We do, too, so we made a whole recipe based on it. It's an easy roasted sweet potato "fry" that you dip in Lime Crème Fraîche (page 41) before dipping again into either Garlic Toast Crunchies or Cinnamon Toast Crunchies (page 37). The crème fraîche acts like glue for the crumbs to adhere to. You can make just one of the crunchies, but we recommend you do both and switch between salty and sweet. It's, dare we say, the most fun. The potatoes will crisp up more as they cool, and they taste great at room temperature.

2 sweet potatoes (about 1 pound/454 g)

1 tablespoon olive oil

½ teaspoon kosher salt

Freshly ground black pepper

Pinch of cayenne (optional)

FOR SERVING

Lime Crème Fraîche (page 41)

Garlic Toast Crunchies (page 37), and/or Cinnamon Toast Crunchies (page 37)

1 Preheat the oven to 425°F (215°C). Line a large baking sheet with parchment paper.

2 Peel the sweet potatoes (or not!) and cut them into fries about ¼ inch (6 mm) wide and 3 inches (7.5 cm) long.

3 Toss the potatoes with the olive oil, salt, pepper, and cayenne (if using) in a medium bowl until evenly coated. Spread them out in a single layer on the baking sheet.

4 Bake for 15 to 20 minutes, until they are browned on the bottom, and then flip them over and bake for another 10 to 15 minutes, until deeply browned all over.

5 Remove from the oven, and allow to cool for 5 minutes. Serve with the Lime Crème Fraîche and the Garlic and/or Cinnamon Toast Crunchies, and dip, baby, dip.

PREP AHEAD

Make the Lime Crème Fraîche up to 2 weeks in advance. Store in an airtight container in the fridge.

HACKABLE

Sub ¼ cup (55 g) sour cream mixed with a spritz of lime juice for the crème fraîche.

EASY ASPARAGUS
with Fried Capers
serves 2 to 3

This easy one-pan dish takes 10 minutes to make, tops. The pan will seem a little overcrowded when you first add the asparagus, but this is ideal. The steam produced as a result will ensure the stalks are cooked all the way through. This recipe works best with thin asparagus. If the stalks are too thick, they'll taste raw. Omit the Parmesan to make it vegan.

3 tablespoons olive oil

1 bunch thin asparagus (about 1 pound/ 454 g), woody ends trimmed or snapped

Kosher salt and freshly ground black pepper

2 garlic cloves, thinly sliced

Fried Capers (page 36)

2 tablespoons finely grated Parmesan (optional)

1 Heat the olive oil in a large skillet over medium-high heat. Add the asparagus, and cook without moving for 2 minutes. Shake the pan to stir, season with salt and pepper, and continue to cook the asparagus, moving them only to stir in 2-minute intervals, until the asparagus is browned and cooked to your desired tenderness, 2 to 4 minutes more.

2 Reduce the heat to low, add the garlic, and cook until fragrant, about 30 seconds. Be careful not to let the garlic burn.

3 Remove from the heat, and transfer the asparagus to a platter. Top it with the Fried Capers and Parmesan (if using).

KALE SALAD
(Because Everyone Needs to Know How to Make One)

serves 1 to 2

Let it be known that every person who knows their way around a kitchen should be able to make a simple and delicious kale salad on a whim. This one is about as classic as it gets, with shredded lacinato kale, garlicky dressing, and a pile of finely grated Parmesan. We listed the Garlic Toast Crunchies (page 37) as optional, but if you're smart, you'll use them. To spice things up, add a couple dashes of your favorite hot sauce to the dressing in step 1.

3 tablespoons olive oil

3 tablespoons finely grated Parmesan, plus more for serving

1½ tablespoons sherry vinegar

1½ teaspoons Dijon mustard

1 small garlic clove, grated

¾ teaspoon honey

¼ teaspoon kosher salt

Freshly ground black pepper

1 bunch lacinato kale (about 6.5 ounces/ 184 g), large ribs removed

Garlic Toast Crunchies (page 37; optional)

1 Whisk together the olive oil, Parmesan, vinegar, Dijon, garlic, honey, salt, and a bunch of pepper in a small bowl until emulsified into a dressing.

2 Stack the kale leaves, roll them into a cigar, and thinly slice them to create ribbons. Transfer to a large salad bowl, and toss with half of the dressing. Add more salt, pepper, and dressing to taste. (Any leftover dressing can be used for another kale salad.) At this point, the salad can sit at room temperature for up to 1 hour.

3 Top with the Garlic Toast Crunchies (if using) and more Parmesan just before serving.

PREP AHEAD
Make the dressing up to 4 days in advance and store in an airtight container in the fridge. Prep and store the kale in an airtight container in the fridge up to 2 days in advance.

MINT CHIP MILKSHAKE

serves 1 to 2

Milkshakes rule because they feel deeply luxurious yet homey and comforting at the same time. You've probably already put this together, but you can make this milkshake with any flavor ice cream you want. You could even use nut milk and dairy-free ice cream for a vegan version or add a splash of booze, if you are so inclined. Just to be clear, this is by far the easiest recipe in the book.

1 pint (454 g) mint chip ice cream
⅓ cup (80 ml) whole milk
Whipped cream and crushed Thin Mints, for serving (optional)

1 Scoop the ice cream into a blender, pour the milk on top, and blend until smooth. If you'd like it to be thinner, blend in more milk, a couple tablespoons at a time.

2 Pour into a milkshake glass, and top with whipped cream and crushed cookies (if using).

SPECIAL EQUIPMENT
Blender

STRAWBERRY LAVA CAKE FOR TWO

serves 2

According to strawberry folklore, if you ever share a strawberry with someone, you are bound to fall in love, which basically makes this dessert a love potion. Be careful who you eat it with. If you don't have a 10-ounce (300 ml) ramekin (which is about 4 inches/10 cm in diameter), bake this in two 6-ounce (180 ml) ones. You'll need to reduce the bake time by a couple minutes if you do. The trickiest part is inverting the cake while it's still hot without burning yourself or accidentally breaking it open and spilling the molten filling. If you opt to serve it straight from the ramekin instead, we won't judge you. And don't worry, if you accidentally overbake it, it will still be quite tasty; it just won't be molten. The food coloring is optional, but the cake will be a weird, flesh-toned color if you don't use it, and nobody wants that, not even if you just shared a strawberry with them.

3 tablespoons unsalted butter, plus more for the ramekin

2 tablespoons all-purpose flour, plus more for the ramekin

2 ounces (57 g) white chocolate, chopped (about ⅓ cup)

3 tablespoons good-quality strawberry preserves

¼ teaspoon kosher salt

1 egg

1 egg yolk

About 3 drops red food coloring (optional)

Thinly sliced strawberries and confectioners' sugar, for serving

1 Preheat the oven to 400°F (200°C). Butter the inside of a 10-ounce (300 ml) ramekin, and dust the buttered ramekin with flour, making sure every bit of the interior is covered. Set aside.

2 Heat the white chocolate, strawberry preserves, and butter in a small pot over low heat, stirring constantly, until the butter and chocolate have melted and the mixture is fully combined, 2 to 3 minutes. Remove from the heat, and stir in the salt.

3 Whisk the egg and egg yolk vigorously in a medium bowl until the mixture is pale and very thick, about 2 minutes. Whisk in the flour.

4 Gently stir the chocolate-strawberry mixture into the egg mixture until fully combined. Stir in the food coloring (if using). Pour the mixture into the ramekin.

5 Bake for about 16 minutes, until the edges are set and the cake is slightly puffed but the center is still quite soft and a little jiggly. Remove from the oven and let cool slightly.

6 While the cake is still hot, run a small knife or offset spatula around the edge of the ramekin to loosen. Place a plate over the top of the ramekin, and carefully invert it to release the cake. Use tongs or a kitchen towel to remove the ramekin.

7 Arrange the strawberry slices on top, dust with a little confectioners' sugar, and serve.

PREP AHEAD

Make the base through step 4 up to 2 weeks in advance and freeze. Bake from frozen, adding 5 to 10 minutes to the bake time. If the top of the cake browns too quickly before it's done, cover it lightly with foil.

SPECIAL EQUIPMENT

One 10-ounce (300 ml) ramekin or two 6-ounce (180 ml) ramekins

FREEZABLE

EARL GREY CREAMSICLE POSSETS

serves 2

After Courtney tested this recipe for the first time, her notes said, "My God, these were so good. Was not expecting the goodness level to be so high." To achieve optimum goodness level, don't skimp on the Cinnamon Toast Crunchies (page 37); they make all the difference. These will last for up to 4 days, covered tightly, in the fridge, so feel free to double the recipe if you think you'll eat them in time. With a goodness level this high, you probably will.

1 cup (240 ml) heavy cream
⅓ cup (67 g) sugar
Zest and juice of 1 tangerine
2 Earl Grey tea bags
2 tablespoons fresh lemon juice
Cinnamon Toast Crunchies (page 37)

1 Add the heavy cream, sugar, tangerine zest, and tea bags to a medium pot, and set over medium-high heat. Reduce to a low simmer and cook, stirring occasionally, to thicken slightly, about 5 minutes.

2 Pour the mixture through a fine-mesh sieve into a small pitcher, pressing lightly on the tea bag to extract the liquid.

3 Stir in the lemon juice and 1 tablespoon tangerine juice. (Drink any leftover tangerine juice.)

4 Divide the mixture between two 6-ounce (180 ml) ramekins (or teacups—so cute!), and let them set in the fridge for at least 2 hours.

5 Top with a handful of Cinnamon Toast Crunchies, and serve.

PREP AHEAD
Make the possets up to 4 days in advance. Cover tightly and store in the fridge. Make the Cinnamon Toast Crunchies up to 1 month in advance. Store in an airtight container in the fridge.

SPECIAL EQUIPMENT
Fine-mesh sieve

tiny party plans
spilling tea with your bestie

Give a gossipy evening with your best friend the respect it deserves by devoting an entire party to it. If spilling the tea doesn't do it for you, there are plenty of other ways to pass the time. Analyze each other's dreams, plan a convention, watch *The Mole* (not the most current one; the one from 2001 that's hosted by Anderson Cooper), or do nothing at all but sit in silence and meditate on the slurping sounds that result from eating Fettuccine Rancho Alfredo. This party works great as a facetime, too.

menu

Fettuccine Rancho Alfredo (page 191), Kale Salad (Because Everyone Needs to Know How to Make One; page 204), Earl Grey Creamsicle Possets (page 211), a really great bottle of wine (make it a juicy red to go along with all the juicy gossip), and some garlic bread.

dress

Wear fancy hats and gloves. If you happen to smoke, use one of those long cigarette holder thingies. But also, don't smoke, kids.

ambiance

Serve whatever you are drinking in pretty porcelain teacups, if you have them. Go hard on the tea party vibes.

playlist suggestions

Songs about gossip, rumors, and minding your own business: "I Heard It Through the Grapevine" by Marvin Gaye, "Til I Hear It From You" by the Gin Blossoms, "Rumors" by Club Nouveau, "None of Your Business" by Salt-N-Pepa, "Mind Your Own Business" by Delta 5, "I Heard a Rumour" by Bananarama, and the entirety of Fleetwood Mac's hit album, *Rumours*.

prep plan

one day out: Make the Garlic Toast Crunchies for the salad and the Cinnamon Toast Crunchies for the possets; make the Ramen Ranch Seasoning for the fettuccine; make the possets.

morning of the party: Make the salad dressing and prep the kale.

when your guest arrives: Pop the wine and heat and serve the garlic bread.

just before dinner: Make the fettuccine, toss the salad, and serve.

after dinner: Serve the possets.

date night

Date nights need no introduction: They are a tale as old as time, so draft an invite to your main squeeze or crush du jour, slip into something a little more comfortable, and smash that send button. The hardest part is over; all you gotta do now is, ahem . . . cook. We encourage you to Lady and the Tramp the fajitas; it's not quite the same as with spaghetti, but with enough tenacity and the right approach, it could work. Some people (our editors) called us crazy for adding beans to a date-night menu. But we say, if you can endure the consequences of eating the musical fruit with the one you love, then the two of you just might be marriage material.

menu

Chips and salsa; Fajitas for Two (page 192); Delicious Beans!!! (page 199); Strawberry Lava Cake for Two (page 208); beer, wine, or margaritas.

prep plan

two days out: Soak the beans.

one day out: Marinate the steak for the fajitas and make the Pico de Gallo (if using); cook the beans.

morning of the party: Prep the mise en place for the fajitas.

when your guest arrives: Make the margaritas or serve the beer and wine along with chips and salsa.

just before dinner: Cook the fajitas, reheat the beans, and serve.

after dinner: Make the lava cake…together.

ambiance

Make it fun and sexy, whatever that means to you.

dress

See above, re: ambiance.

playlist suggestions

See above, re: dress.

social hangover, party of one

There comes a time in every party person's life when we must party alone. Not because we have to, but because we want to. Social hangovers are real, and it's okay—healthy even—to step away from the crowd from time to time. That doesn't mean the party has to end. Your entire life can be a party if you treat it right, so lather yourself up with some self-love, and let your party of one begin.

menu

Low-Baked Salmon in Miso Butter (page 195), Chilled Tofu with Sesame Spinach (page 196); Mint Chip Milkshake (page 207). Drink whatever your heart desires: Sake, beer, cherry cola, flat water—it's all for you.

prep plan

morning of the party: Make the tofu; make the Miso Butter for the salmon.

literally whenever you want: Drink your bevvies; make the salmon; make the milkshake, and serve with the tofu.

ambiance

Stream your favorite playlist, movie, or TV show as loud as you want. Do a little dance in your living room. Play "the floor is lava." Jump on the bed. Do literally whatever you want.

dress

Totally up to you, but probably a fabulous caftan or some sort of silk smoking jacket with hot pants and bunny slippers.

playlist suggestions

Smooth, soothing tones that can lift your spirit. Things like Clairo, Hall & Oates, Saya Gray, or Kacey Musgraves.

theme parties

Theme parties are, by far, Brie and Courtney's favorite type of get-together. If it weren't for the maximum page count of this book, we'd probably have included at least ten more. There's just something special about creating a fully formed party where all the details play off of each other, from the food to the dress to the decorations and even the entertainment. It completes us. Now, let it complete you.

we're hot for hot dogs

The Hot Dog Appreciation Club was born on the night of January 12, 2019, when Courtney drunkenly took to her Instagram stories, explaining that late-night hot dogs are the best. "Nothing is better than coming home to a warm wiener in a flour tortilla with ketchup and mustard and pickled serranos" is what she said, specifically. Pretty much everyone agreed, so she made official Hot Dog Appreciation Club badges and mailed them to anyone who DM'ed her and requested to join. The only requirement was that they had to appreciate hot dogs. Brie is a person who deeply appreciates hot dogs, so it's no surprise that she was among the first to come aboard. The club was wildly popular, and plans for a festival commenced. Cut to May 15, 2020. All pandemics aside, it was a typical day in Los Angeles, sunny with a high of 77°F (25°C). Some would call it perfect, but there was nothing perfect about it, for this was the day we discovered the one thing that could tear us apart. Up to this point, we hadn't thought it could happen. We never knew, because we never asked. Maybe, in our own way, we were afraid of what the answer might be. It started simply enough, when Brie posed two simple questions to our group text thread (which was named "Party People," by the way): "Is a hot dog a sandwich? Is cereal a soup?" Of course cereal isn't soup; everyone knows that. Soup must be broth based, we all agreed. But when it came to whether a hot dog is a sandwich, well, that's when the relish hit the fan.

We were a group divided, with each of us at opposite helms. On one end was Courtney, who emphatically believes that hot dogs are sandwiches, and on the other end, Brie (plus a few others) was absolutely positive that they aren't. We agreed to disagree. We moved on. Years passed. No one breathed "hot dogs" and "sandwiches" in the same sentence again. Then, in the fall of 2024, the Sandwich Wars reignited.

Faye

connected bun? not a sammy

monique

Faye, you're poking a hornets nest

Kate

this is my thought: I think a hot dog is not a sandwich because it's good enough to have its own category
Plus I'm not getting sandwiches at a baseball games- hotdog just looks better as a word even and can make better cartoon graphics

B L

I'm sick

Not this again

> Kate you make an excellent point. But by calling a hot dog a sandwich, you aren't taking away the hot dog-ness of it. It's kind of like saying all squares are rectangles, but not all rectangles are squares

> All hot dogs are sandwiches, but not all sandwiches are hot dog

B L

I hate you

> Jajahhahahahahahahababa

> It's like Sandwich is the genus and cheeseburger is the species

monique

can we pick this one up after the election is over?

Faye

it should really be on the ballot

Meanwhile, the Hot Dog Appreciation Club was going strong. Its gregarious facade masked the turmoil bubbling in its ranks. Brie's mom volunteered her house as ground zero for the club's annual festival. As far as the outside world knew, everything was dandy. And the outside world was right, because that's the power of hot dogs. Even when they divide us, they unite us. Nothing beats hanging in the sunshine and scarfing down wieners all day. They are ubiquitous at backyard barbecues. They are found in every ballpark across the nation. Babies eat them. Grandparents eat them. Children as young as eight years old douse them in an ungodly amount of black pepper and watch with wonder as their parents pretend to enjoy them. Even fully grown adult women drunkenly take to social media to proclaim their love for them from time to time.

And it doesn't matter whether it's a frank, a wiener, a coney, a footlong, a sausage, a glizzy, or even a sandwich. Whatever you call it, we challenge you to find a person who wouldn't happily eat one.

B L

I stand behind if you said "can you pick me up a sandwich?" I would not get you a hotdog

> But if you asked for a sandwich and you got a hot dog, would you turn it down?

Laura

Hehe Courtney

LM

Never

B L

Omg Courtney true

I love hot dogs

They are so cute!

Laura

They are the best food

Our festival has grown every year, and we intend to keep it that way. We get as many different types of hot dogs as we can—all the typical brands (yes, even the plant-based ones), plus fancy varieties from specialty butchers and hot dog purveyors from all over the country—then we fire up the grill and put out every condiment our hearts could dream of (see page 28). There's Aperol Negroni Melons (page 224), Pickle Coleslaw (page 231), Super-Fine Hot Dog Chili (page 228) for chili dogs, Chile con Queso (a Love Story; page 118), and of course, dessert. In 2024, we served the Party People Pop-Tart Peach Pie (PPP-TPP; page 106), and she was the belle of the ball. Our friends donate food or drink to the cause, too. One of them always makes a hot dog pizza; another brings hot dog–shaped cookies; one friend even brought a nine-foot inflatable hot dog. She was late that day because she inflated it by herself without an air pump, and it took her 4 hours. Then she couldn't fit it in her car. By God, she made it, though. Brie's dad hosts a raucous hot dog trivia session via megaphone while donning a hot dog suit, and her mom organizes all the ingredients, invites, decorations, and yard games. There's even a photo booth. To say it's one of the days we look forward to the most is putting it mildly. Now, more than ever, we need hot dogs. We need to appreciate them, we need to eat them, and we need to enjoy them with our party people. If you'd like to join the Hot Dog Appreciation Club, please dial 1-866-PRTY-PPL. Operators are standing by.

playlist suggestions

Songs about America! Freedom! And dogs! Also "Tropical Hotdog Night" by Captain Beefheart and his Magic Band.

menu

Aperol Negroni Melons (page 224); hot dogs with all the condiments (see page 227); Super-Fine Hot Dog Chili (page 228); Pickle Coleslaw (page 231); May We Present: The Hot Dog Sandwich, a Bridge to a Better Tomorrow (page 232); Chile con Queso (a Love Story; page 118); cold beers; and dessert (dealer's choice). Tell your friends to donate to the cause, too.

prep plan

three days out: Decide which condiments you want to offer (you probably want to make all of them), and plan to make them as far in advance as possible.

two days out: Make any condiments you can, plus the Comeback Sauce for the hot dog sandwiches; make the melons and freeze, if freezing.

one day out: Make the coleslaw; make the chili; set up decorations (if using); stage serving utensils, platters, plates, and napkins; set up as much of the bar area as possible.

morning of the party: Make any remaining condiments and the queso; make the dessert.

as guests arrive: Set out drinks and ice at the bar area; set out the melons; reheat the queso and serve.

throughout the party: Cook the hot dogs, ideally on the grill, otherwise via your preferred method; reheat the chili and serve with the hot dogs along with all the condiments; assemble and griddle the hot dog sandwiches; serve the dessert.

ambiance

Best held outside with yard games, shady trees, hot dog trivia, giant inflatable hot dogs, a swimming pool, and dachshunds.

dress

Anything and everything hot dog related. There is no wrong answer.

APEROL NEGRONI MELONS

serves 8 as a party snack

Not only is this snack great for hot dog parties, it's lovely for all al fresco dining adventures. It's also a great way to catch a buzz while remaining hydrated thanks to the melon's extra water content. What we're trying to say is, this just might be the perfect party food. Instead of Campari, which is the traditional Negroni ingredient, we use Aperol. It's less bitter and doesn't overwhelm the delicate flavor of the melon. If it's really hot out, pop them in the freezer for at least 4 hours before serving for A+ popsicle vibes.

4 ounces (120 ml) Aperol

4 ounces (120 ml) gin

4 ounces (120 ml) sweet vermouth

1 small melon, such as cantaloupe or mini watermelon

1   Combine the Aperol, gin, and vermouth in a small pitcher, and set aside.

2   Cut the melon in half and remove the seeds, if necessary. Working over a bowl to save the juice, use a melon baller or a spoon to scoop the flesh into bite-size chunks. Transfer the melon chunks and juice to a large, double-lined zipper-top bag, and pour the Aperol Negroni mixture over them. Store in the fridge for at least 4 hours, tossing every hour to make sure all the melon chunks have equal access to the Negroni.

3   Strain the melon chunks into a bowl, and serve chilled. You could also arrange them on a cute little platter with frilly toothpicks. Pour the leftover juice into shot glasses and serve it ice-cold on the side.

FREEZABLE

SPECIAL EQUIPMENT
Melon baller, frilly toothpicks, shot glasses

PREP AHEAD
Make up to 4 days in advance and store in an airtight container in the fridge or freeze for up to 1 month.

THE FINE ART OF COOKING HOT DOGS

Welcome to our magnum opus. If you skipped straight to this page, then you are a true Party Person, and we salute you. All the cooking methods below result in delicious dogs, but we prefer the grill and stovetop methods best. There's one method you won't find here, and that's the microwave. Avoid it at all costs, unless you like rubbery weenies. Plan for 2½ hot dogs per person (so a party of eight gets 20 hot dogs, a party of ten gets 25 dogs, and so on). And don't worry about scoring or pricking them first; it's simply not necessary.

ON THE GRILL

Heat the grill to medium. Add the hot dogs, and grill for about 4 minutes, rotating every minute or so, until they are browned, plump, and a little charred. Put them on the grill at an angle to the grate, and only move them to rotate them to a new side to get those cool-looking grill marks.

BOILED

Bring a large pot of water (or beer for better flavor!) to a boil over high heat. Add the hot dogs, and boil until they are plump, about 5 minutes. Remove from the pot, and drain on paper towels.

ON THE STOVETOP

Melt ½ tablespoon butter in a large skillet over medium heat. When the butter foams and then subsides, add the hot dogs and sear on all sides until they are plumped up and browned, 2 to 3 minutes. (Do this in batches if you are making a lot of dogs, adding more butter to the pan as needed.)

ON A STICK

Light a fire, and thread a hot dog onto a metal skewer or a cleaned wire hanger. Hold it over the flame, rotating it often, until it's cooked through and a little burnt, about 3 minutes.

IN THE OVEN

Preheat the oven to 400°F (200°C). Place the hot dogs on a rimmed baking sheet or in a baking dish, and roast for about 10 minutes, until they have plumped up and browned.

LET'S TALK BUNS

If you are grilling the dogs, throw the buns on the grill, too. Open them up and lay them cut side down on the grill until toasted, about 30 seconds. If you're feeling fancy, brush the insides with some melted Miso Butter (page 42) first.

To steam buns, preheat the oven to 325°F (165°C). Wet your hands and use your fingers to flick a fine mist of water onto a large baking sheet. Place the buns in a single layer on the sheet, and mist their tops with a small amount of water, too. Cover the baking sheet tightly with foil, and place it in the oven for about 10 minutes, until the buns are warmed through and soft. Don't use too much water, or they will get soggy. You want just enough to create a small amount of steam in the oven.

RE: CONDIMENTS

Remember this golden hot dog rule: People come for the dogs, but they stay for the condiments. Literally every recipe in our condiment section (starting on page 28) will taste great on a doggie, but don't forget the basics like ketchup, mustard, and mayo. Potato chips, corn chips, sauerkraut, and pickled peppers are also a good idea. Really there's no wrong way to do condiments, as long as you give the people what they want, and they want plenty of options. Have fun with it.

SUPER-FINE HOT DOG CHILI

makes enough for about 20 hot dogs

This hot dog chili is so quick, so easy, and sooooo fine, because you are gonna break it up with a sturdy spoon as it cooks to achieve an extremely pulverized, minced texture. That's the best kind of chili for a hot dog. To be clear, this is not a recipe for chili you would eat out of a bowl, and we aren't trying to submit it to any chili cook-offs. This is a down-and-dirty chili for hot dogs. And it gets the job done. For more spice, add some cayenne. For less spice, cut the jalapeños.

2 tablespoons olive oil

1 medium yellow onion, finely chopped

2 medium jalapeños, seeded and finely chopped

Kosher salt

4 garlic cloves, thinly sliced

2 tablespoons chili powder

1 tablespoon garlic powder

1 tablespoon ground cumin

1 pound (454 g) 80% lean ground beef

¼ cup (70 g) tomato paste

1½ cups (360 ml) stock (beef, chicken, or veggie), or water

1 Heat the olive oil in a large pot or Dutch oven over medium-high heat. Add the onion and jalapeños, season with salt, and cook until the onions are see-through, about 5 minutes.

2 Add the garlic, chili powder, garlic powder, and cumin (it's a lot, we know, but it adds so much flavor!), and cook until fragrant, about 1 minute.

3 Add the ground beef, season with salt, and cook until browned, 8 to 10 minutes. Use a sturdy wooden spoon or spatula to constantly break up the meat into a super-fine mince as it cooks. Just chop, chop, chop away. The finer the better. We want this chili to be soooooo fine.

4 Stir in the tomato paste, and cook until it darkens, about 1 minute. Stir in the stock, and bring to a simmer. Reduce the heat to low, cover, and simmer, stirring occasionally, until it's a thick, spoonable consistency—something you'd like to be piled on top of a hot dog—about 30 minutes. Skim the oil from the top, if you wanna. Taste and add more salt if needed.

5 To serve, simply spoon some chili on top of a hot dog and add any other condiments you like. Not ketchup, though. Don't you dare.

FREEZABLE

PREP AHEAD
Make the chili up to 5 days in advance. Store in an airtight container in the fridge or freeze for up to 1 month.

PICKLE COLESLAW

serves 8

This coleslaw has pickles *inside* it. That's right, the pickles are coming from *inside the coleslaw*, and there's nothing scary about it. Grate the pickles on the large side of a box grater, and be sure to use whole pickles or spears. (Sliced pickles would be a real pain to shred.) Dill pickles make for a savory slaw; use bread and butter pickles for something sweeter; and if pickles aren't your thing, sauerkraut or shredded kimchi would be great, too. Add the scallions to taste, depending on how much you like onions.

1 medium head green cabbage

1 large carrot, grated on a bias

1 to 3 scallions, thinly sliced on a bias

1 cup (150 g) grated dill pickles

2 teaspoons kosher salt, plus more to taste

½ cup (110 g) mayonnaise

3 tablespoons fresh lemon juice

2 tablespoons apple cider vinegar

2 tablespoons sugar

1 tablespoon Dijon mustard

2 teaspoons Louisiana-style hot sauce

Freshly ground black pepper

1 Quarter the cabbage, core it, and slice each quarter into very thin ribbons. You should have about 16½ cups (650 g) shredded cabbage. Add the massive amount of cabbage to a massively large bowl, along with the carrot, scallions, and pickles. Add the salt, and toss to combine.

2 Whisk together the mayo, lemon juice, vinegar, sugar, Dijon, and hot sauce in a small bowl, and pour it over the cabbage mixture. Toss and season with more salt, if needed, plus lots of black pepper. Store in the fridge for at least 1 hour before serving.

PREP AHEAD

Make the coleslaw up to 3 days in advance. It will release water as it sits; strain it off as needed.

THE HOT DOG SANDWICH
a Bridge to a Better Tomorrow

makes 1 sandwich

Yes, we know that the hot dog/sandwich debate is a little tired at this point, but ... *is* a hot dog a sandwich? While the answer is most certainly yes, some other people who are attached to this book disagree. In the interest of reaching across the aisle, we've decided to create this bipartisan recipe that is basically a Reuben, but with hot dogs. Really, any sandwich can be a hot dog sandwich: A club, a Cuban, a dip, a banh mi, or even a chopped cheese made with hot dogs would all be delicious. It just goes to show that there's no problem that can't be solved with an open mind and a lot of love. You may say we're dreamers, but we aren't the only ones. Just imagine all the hot dog sandwiches.

½ tablespoon unsalted butter

2 hot dogs, butterflied lengthwise almost all the way through but still connected at the skin

1 tablespoon unsalted butter, softened

2 slices Jewish rye bread

¼ cup (55 g) Comeback Sauce (page 40)

2 slices Swiss cheese

⅓ cup (65 g) drained sauerkraut, warmed

Pickles

Potato chips (optional)

1   Heat the butter in a medium skillet over medium-high heat. When it foams and subsides, add the hot dogs, cut side down. Press down on them with a flat spatula, and cook on one side until browned, about 1 minute. Flip and cook on the other side until they are browned and beginning to curl, about 1 minute. Transfer the hot dogs to a paper towel–lined plate. When it's cool enough, wipe out the skillet with another paper towel.

2   Spread the softened butter on one side of each slice of the bread, and lay the slices, buttered side down, on a clean plate or work surface. Spread the Comeback Sauce on the non-buttered side of each slice, and add a piece of Swiss cheese to one of the slices. Place the butterflied hot dogs on top of the cheese. Top with the sauerkraut, followed by the second slice of Swiss cheese, and then close the sandwich with the other slice of bread, Comeback Sauce side down.

3   Griddle the sandwich in the wiped-out skillet over medium-low heat until the bread toasts and the cheese melts, about 2 minutes per side. Cover the pan, if needed, to help the cheese melt more quickly.

4   Slice the sandwich in half on the diagonal, stuff it with some pickles and potato chips, if using, and serve.

PREP AHEAD
Make the Comeback Sauce up to 1 month in advance. Store in an airtight container in the fridge.

HACKABLE
Use store-bought Thousand Island dressing instead of the Comeback Sauce.

the breakfast club

One hot summer weekend, we road-tripped down to Valle de Guadalupe with our friends Erin and Mo for a joint birthday celebration. It's a quick-and-easy jaunt from Los Angeles: four hours down I-5 and across the border into Mexican wine country. Or so we thought. Brie swung by and picked up the rest of us from Courtney's house in Silver Lake. As everyone piled in, Erin asked if we had our passports. She was joking, of course, because we all had our passports. Besides deciding where we'd eat, the only other thing we'd spoken about leading up to the trip was how we could *NOT FORGET OUR PASSPORTS.* It was at this point that Brie realized she had forgotten her passport. At the time, Brie lived in Malibu. For those of you unfamiliar with the geography of Los Angeles, she may as well have lived on the moon. We weren't going to leave her, and we didn't want to risk getting stuck at the border, so off to Malibu we went. Upon arrival, Brie ran in to grab her passport, which was stashed in her safe. Except when she got there, her safe was locked. "No big deal. All safes are locked," is probably what you are thinking. But you'd be wrong, because hers was a digital safe . . . and the battery had died. We tried breaking in, to no avail. Turns out, safes are extremely effective at preventing break-ins. By now, we began to wonder if this was some sort of omen. Maybe we shouldn't go on this trip. Maybe something was trying to prevent us from traveling. As Mo began to explain why we should call the whole thing off, Brie found her passport. It was in a backpack in her closet.

Back on the road we hopped; we were several hours behind schedule and worried we would miss our dinner reservation, but the trip was on, baby! We jammed out to Enigma and Paula Cole, ate gas station hot dogs, and flew down the interstate. At about the halfway point, there was a moment of silence. The music stopped, and no one was talking. It was as if the proverbial clouds had parted, because it got quiet just in time for Courtney, who was driving, to overhear Brie in the passenger seat say, "I just want to see one alien, one time." Brie did not say this to the group; she said it quietly to herself, in almost a whisper, as she looked out the window and off into the clouds. If there had been any other noise in the car, Courtney would have missed it. After confirming that Brie did, in fact, say that, the phrase "one alien, one time" was immediately added to the group's vernacular. (We have an entire book of idioms at this point, including but not limited to "the littlest mermaid," "jingle bell mazel tov," "we

did it again!" and "messipe," but those are all stories for another time.)

We finally crossed the border and were getting closer to our hotel. We had made up some time, and all signs pointed to yes when it came to making our dinner reservation. Thank God, because gas station hot dogs can only take you so far. That's when we noticed the smoke. Billows of plumes filled the air as we drove into multiple small-scale, yet serious, wildfires. By the time we got to the hotel, a message was waiting for us: Due to the fires, our dinner reservation had been cancelled. So in lieu of dinner that night, we hung out under the stars and kept our eyes peeled for UFOs. We just needed to see *one* alien, *one* time, after all. The next morning, we woke up to great news. The fires were out, no one was injured, and the restaurant would be open that night with seats saved for us.

menu

Iced Coffee Martinis (page 238), Mixed Citrus Palomas (page 241), Breakfast Taco Casserole (page 245), Hotcakes de Elote a la Doña Esthela (page 242), lots of fresh fruit.

dress

Cozy PJs and comfy robes. Hair curlers encouraged.

ambiance

Soft morning light, newspapers, comics, notebooks and writing utensils for early morning journaling. Crossword puzzles, Wordles, and sudoku. Saturday morning cartoons playing in the background.

prep plan

two days out: Make the martini base; make the Delicious Beans!!! for the casserole (if using); make the Lime Crème Fraîche for the hotcakes (if using).

one day out: Make the paloma base; make the Pico de Gallo for the casserole (if using); make the casserole through step 4; set up decorations (if using); stage serving utensils, platters, plates, and napkins; set up as much of the bar area as possible.

morning of the party: Make the hotcakes batter; assemble the fruit platter.

as guests arrive: Set out the palomas, martinis, and ice at the bar area; set out the fruit platter.

just before eating: Top and bake the casserole; reheat the beans (if using); set out the fixins for the casserole; griddle and serve the hotcakes.

playlist suggestions

Songs about morning-time, like "Wake Me Up Before You Go-Go" by Wham!, "Good Morning Friend" by Johnny Cash, "Some Velvet Morning" by Nancy Sinatra and Lee Hazlewood, and "In the Morning of the Magicians" by The Flaming Lips. Plus the soundtrack to *The Breakfast Club*.

After some incredible in-room massages, it seemed like the day couldn't possibly improve, but then again, we hadn't eaten breakfast yet. We drove 30 minutes southwest to La Cocina de Doña Esthela. Upon arrival, it looked more like a ranch than a restaurant, complete with farm animals. The wait was long, but we were mighty. We ordered the tacos dorados, borrego tatemado, chilaquiles verdes, machaca quesatacos, and hotcakes de elote, all for the table to share. (We were hungry, but also, as Courtney says, "It's my *job* to taste everything.") As soon as the food hit the table, it became clear: *This* was the reason we had come to Valle de Guadalupe. Every dish was better than the last. The chilaquiles were crispy *and* chewy, with a bright salsa verde and velvety refried beans to match. The earthy, smoky borrego tatemado, when scooped with a warm, house-made corn tortilla, was almost impossible to beat. But there was a clear winner: the hotcakes de elote. Freshly griddled on the comal, these fluffy clouds were so jam-packed with the flavor of fresh, sweet corn, we didn't even need the maple syrup. You could taste the love that went into them, and it melted our hearts, just like the butter that oozed over their warm, crisp edges. We never did see any extraterrestrials on that trip, but that meal was out of this world, and to this day, we all agree it was the best breakfast any of us have ever had. If you have the means, do yourself a favor and make the trek to La Cocina de Doña Esthela for breakfast. We should all be so lucky to see—and taste—one of those hotcakes at least one time.

But, if you can't make the trek, throw this party instead. Breakfast is the most important meal of the day, so it follows that this party is the most important one in this book.

ICED COFFEE MARTINIS

makes eight 5-ounce (150 ml) cocktails

We swap espresso for cold brew in this classic martini, because few of us have espresso machines at home. Be sure to use cold brew concentrate, the kind you need to water down before drinking. We don't dilute it in this recipe—we want that intense coffee flavor. These are best served up, but on the rocks will work if you don't have a shaker. Use decaf for a caffeine-free version (gasp!).

16 ounces (480 ml) cold brew concentrate

16 ounces (480 ml) vodka

8 ounces (240 ml) coffee liqueur, like Kahlúa

Ice

1 Combine the cold brew concentrate, vodka, and coffee liqueur in an airtight container. Store in the fridge for a least 2 hours and up to a million years.

2 To serve up, fill a cocktail shaker with ice, add 5 ounces (150 ml) of the martini mixture, and shake vigorously until fabulously chilled, about 30 seconds. Strain into a chilled martini glass.

3 To serve on the rocks, fill a rocks glass with ice, pour in 4 ounces (120 ml) of the martini mixture, and stir vigorously for 30 seconds.

FREEZABLE

SPECIAL EQUIPMENT
Cocktail shaker, martini or rocks glasses

PREP AHEAD
Make the martini base up to 1 million years in advance and store in the fridge or freezer.

MIXED CITRUS PALOMAS

makes eight 6-ounce (180 ml) cocktails

Palomas are basically a grapefruit and tequila highball, but in this case, we add various orange juices to kick it up a notch. Orange juice can differ greatly in sweetness, so taste the base before adding the simple syrup. You may find you don't need it at all, or you may want to add a little extra. Keep in mind that club soda will dilute the flavor and sweetness, while grapefruit soda will add a little more sugar.

13 ounces (385 ml) tequila

8 ounces (240 ml) fresh grapefruit juice

8 ounces (240 ml) fresh assorted orange juices, like blood orange, tangerine, clementine, or mandarin

1 ounce (30 ml) fresh lime juice

2 to 3 ounces (60 to 90 ml) simple syrup (optional; see Note)

Chile Lime Salt (page 36)

Ice

16 ounces (480 ml) club soda or grapefruit soda

Lime wedges

1 Combine the tequila, grapefruit juice, mixed orange juices, and lime juice in an airtight container. Add simple syrup (if using) to taste. Store the mix in the fridge for a least 2 hours and up to 3 days.

2 To serve, add the Chile Lime Salt to a small plate. Run a lime wedge around the rim of your paloma glasses to moisten them and then dunk the rims in the salt and fill with ice. Pour 4 ounces (120 ml) of the tequila mixture into each glass, and stir to chill.

3 Top off with club soda or grapefruit soda, and garnish with a lime wedge.

PREP AHEAD
Make the tequila mixture up to 3 days in advance and store in the fridge or in the freezer for up to 1 month. Thaw before serving.

HACKABLE
Use regular salt instead of the Chile Lime Salt.

NOTE
To make simple syrup, combine equal parts water and sugar in a small pot over medium-high heat. Bring to a boil, and give it a quick stir to make sure the sugar has dissolved. Remove from the heat, and cool to room temperature. Or skip it altogether and use store-bought simple syrup. Be sure to use standard 1:1 simple syrup (equal parts sugar and water).

HOTCAKES DE ELOTE A LA DOÑA ESTHELA

serves 6 to 8

Here it is folks: Our version of the hotcakes de elote from Doña Esthela. They could never be exactly the same, but they are still freaking delicious. As far as topping them goes, we like the traditional route of butter and maple syrup, but these can be savory, too—so add some of those Breakfast Taco Casserole (page 245) fixings or even smoked salmon and cream cheese for bagel vibes. This makes about twenty 3- to 4-inch (7.5 to 10 cm) pancakes. As a bonus for all the hard work of grating the corn, boil the cobs to make a corn stock afterward. It's the perfect chowder base.

6 large ears fresh corn, shucked

2 cups (280 g) all-purpose flour

½ cup (100 g) sugar

2½ teaspoons baking powder

1¼ teaspoons kosher salt

2 eggs

¼ cup (60 ml) whole milk

6 tablespoons unsalted butter, melted, plus more for griddling and serving

Lime Crème Fraîche (page 41)

Maple syrup

1 Grate the corn on the large side of a box grater into a large bowl, being sure to grate all the way to the cob and extract as much of the corn milk as you can. Measure out 2¼ cups (600 g) of the grated corn, including the corn milk. Save any leftovers for another use.

2 Whisk together the flour, sugar, baking powder, and salt in another large bowl.

3 Add the eggs, milk, and melted butter to the grated corn mixture, and whisk to combine. Pour the corn mixture into the dry mixture, and stir until just combined. Let the batter sit for 5 minutes before griddling.

4 Heat the oven to 200°F (95°C). Add a couple tablespoons of butter to a large skillet or griddle over medium-high heat. Once the butter foams and subsides, ladle a scant ¼ cup (70 g) batter into the pan. Reduce the heat to medium-low, and cook until the bottom of the hotcakes is set and browned and bubbles rise to the surface and pop, about 1 minute. Flip and cook on the other side until lightly browned, about 1 minute more. Transfer the hotcake to a baking sheet and place in the oven to keep warm. Repeat with the remaining batter, adjusting the heat as necessary so the hotcakes don't burn. Griddled hotcakes will hold in the oven for up to 30 minutes.

5 Serve with pats of butter, Lime Crème Fraîche, and maple syrup on top.

> **PREP AHEAD**
> The hotcake batter can be made up to 1 day in advance and stored in the fridge, but it's best made the same day, up to 4 hours in advance.

BREAKFAST TACO CASSEROLE

serves 8 to 12

This recipe swings more toward Austin than it does to Valle de Guadalupe. Originally, we wanted it to be a straight breakfast taco bar, but those are harder to pull off for a big group, especially if you are also making hotcakes (see page 242). The solve is to make a breakfast taco *casserole*, slice it up, and wrap it in tortillas with all the typical fixings. The best part is that you can make it the night before, so all you need to do in the morning is pop it in the oven. For a true Texas-style breakfast taco experience, flour tortillas are the way to go. If you are lucky enough to have a tortilleria in your hometown, get them from there, especially if they're made with lard—that's the good stuff. (You can use corn tortillas, if you must.) Feel free to sub chorizo for the bacon, or for a veggie version, use sautéed onions, peppers, and mushrooms. P.S. No need to thaw the tots before adding them in step 3.

Butter or pan spray, for greasing

1 pound (454 g) bacon, sliced into ½-inch (1 cm) strips

One 32-ounce (907 g) bag frozen Tater Tots

8 ounces (227 g) Colby-Jack or cheddar, shredded, divided

1 dozen eggs

1 cup (240 ml) whole milk

1 teaspoon kosher salt

Freshly ground black pepper

12 to 16 flour tortillas

FOR SERVING

Sliced avocado (optional)

Chopped fresh cilantro (optional)

Delicious Beans!!! (page 199), warmed (optional)

Pico de Gallo (page 33) or salsa (optional)

1 Preheat the oven to 350°F (180°C). Grease a 9 × 13-inch (23 × 33 cm) baking dish with butter or pan spray.

2 Cook the bacon in a large skillet over medium-low heat until crispy, 10 to 15 minutes. Transfer the bacon to a paper towel–lined plate to drain. (Don't forget to save that bacon fat! See page 27.)

3 Layer the tots evenly along the bottom of the prepared baking dish and then cover them with the bacon and half of the Colby-Jack.

4 Whisk together the eggs, milk, salt, and pepper in a large bowl until smooth and then pour it over the tot mixture.

5 Top with the remaining Colby-Jack, and bake for about 40 minutes, until it's puffed up a little and set and the edges are browned.

6 While the casserole bakes, heat the tortillas: Wet your fingers and use them to flick a little bit of water on top of each tortilla, stack them on top of each other, and wrap them in foil. Place them in the oven for about 10 minutes.

7 Have everyone assemble their own "breakfast tacos" by putting a scoop of the casserole in a tortilla and topping it with some avocado, cilantro, beans, and pico (if using).

PREP AHEAD
Make the beans up to 4 days in advance. Store in the fridge and then warm them on the stovetop over medium heat. Add a little water to thin the beans, if needed. Make the casserole through step 4 the night before. Store in the fridge overnight and then start with step 5 in the morning.

HACKABLE
Use canned beans and store-bought salsa instead of the Delicious Beans!!! and Pico de Gallo.

the perfect mess

In a perfect world, you'd be reading a Pulitzer-worthy essay describing **Perfect Mess parties past**, filled with snapshots of Brie, Courtney, and friends living it up, just like you did with the other two theme parties. But that's not going to happen, because we totally made this one up for the book. (Our editor is fine with this, because apparently we are running out of pages.) The photo on the opposite page was the first time we'd ever "hosted" a Perfect Mess party. In full transparency, we were a little worried about how our friends would react to ruining their clothes in the name of our cookbook.* It was all for naught, though, because we had a blast, and, dare we say, it was the most fun photo shoot setup of them all. We can't wait to do it again, but for real this time. The menu is composed of the messiest finger foods imaginable, with no napkins or plates on offer, and the guests should wear all white. The clothes don't need to be fancy by any means—a cheap white T-shirt and sweatpants will do. The idea is to get as stained as possible: Everyone should think of their outfit as a blank canvas, because this party is basically an art project. It's not a food fight at all; it's a peaceful protest against the need for perfection. Just serve the food, and the mess will take care of itself.

* For those who hate the idea of staining their clothes, here's a tip: distilled white vinegar. Put it in a squeeze bottle, drench the stain with it, and hang your clothes out in the sun to dry. Repeat until the stain is gone—it shouldn't take more than 2 or 3 times—and then wash the clothes to get the vinegar out. It's nature's bleach!

ambiance

Definitely outside, ideally somewhere with access to a hose. Tinge some water with food dye, and fill balloons and water guns with it to get the mess going at full tilt.

menu

Doritos Canapés (page 250), The Stickiest Wings (page 253), Pork Ribs with Swayze Sauce (page 254), Cucumber Salad Boats (page 257), Spumoni Ice Cream Cake (page 258), Sparkling Pink Lemonade (page 57), red wine, Kool-Aid, or any drink that has staining power, preferably in coupe or martini glasses that are filled to the brim.

dress

Anything at all, as long as it's all white.

prep plan

three days out: Make the aioli for the canapés; make the Swayze Sauce.

two days out: Make the lemonade base (if using); make the ice cream cake.

one day out: Set up decorations (if using); stage serving platters, but do *not* stage utensils, plates or napkins, because you aren't using any; set up as much of the bar area as possible; marinate the wings and make the sauce; make the ribs through step 4.

morning of the party: Prepare all the mise en place for the salad boats and canapés.

as guests arrive: Set out the drinks and ice at the bar; assemble and serve the canapés.

during the party: Fry the wings; finish and serve the ribs; assemble and serve the cucumber boats; slice and serve the cake.

playlist suggestions

Disco of course! Chic, Donna Summer, and the like.

DORITOS CANAPÉS

serves 8 as a party snack

Nothing messes up fingers like the orange residue from nacho cheese Doritos, except maybe Cheetos, but those are harder to make canapés out of. These don't hold well, so assemble them in small batches and replenish the platter as needed. For those who don't like fish, omit the lox. Use a mandoline to make quick work of slicing the radish and cucumber.

1 party-size (14.5-ounce/411 g) bag nacho cheese Doritos

4 ounces (113 g) lox (optional)

1 bunch radishes, sliced ⅛-inch-thick (3 mm)

2 or 3 Persian cucumbers, sliced ⅛-inch-thick (3 mm)

Pepperoncini Aioli (page 40)

One 2-ounce (57 g) container fish roe or caviar (if you're fancy; optional)

1 Arrange the prettiest Doritos in the bag on a large serving platter.

2 Place a small piece of lox (if using) on top of each Dorito, and add a slice or two of radish and cucumber on the lox.

3 Top with a dollop of Pepperoncini Aioli and a tiny spoonful of roe (if using), and serve.

SPECIAL EQUIPMENT
Mandoline

PREP AHEAD
Make the Pepperoncini Aioli up to 1 month in advance. Store in an airtight container in the fridge.

HACKABLE
Use plain mayo instead of the Pepperoncini Aioli, and top with pepperoncini slices.

THE STICKIEST WINGS

sserves 8 as a party snack

This recipe is based on classic Vietnamese fish sauce wings and adjusted slightly for ease. The reduced fish sauce glaze coats the wings with a salty-sweet umami flavor. It will also coat anything it touches in gooey, funky goodness. Too bad there won't be any napkins to clean up with! Be careful when frying, because the oil will spit, and if the wings you use are extra large, pierce one with a knife after frying it to make sure it's cooked through. If the juices are clear, you are good to go. If not, pop them back in the fryer for another minute or two. For a less pungent wing, omit the reduced fish sauce in steps 7 and 8. Simply top the wings with the shallots and scallions and serve with the lime wedges.

¾ cup (180 ml) fish sauce

¾ cup (150 g) sugar

¾ teaspoon garlic powder

¾ teaspoon onion powder

3 pounds (1.4 kg) chicken wings, separated into drumettes and wingettes

Canola or vegetable oil, for frying

1 cup (180 g) white rice flour

2 tablespoons all-purpose flour

2 tablespoons cornstarch

1 teaspoon baking powder

1 teaspoon sriracha (optional)

FOR SERVING

Frizzled Shallots (page 35)

Thinly sliced scallions

Lime wedges

1 Combine the fish sauce, sugar, garlic powder, onion powder, and ¾ cup (180 ml) hot water in a small container, and mix vigorously until the sugar dissolves.

2 Add the chicken wings to a large zipper-top bag (double bag it to be safe), and pour half of the fish sauce mixture over them. You might feel it's not enough marinade, but it is. Seal the bag, and squish it around to combine. (The squishing is what makes it enough.) Store in the fridge for at least 8 hours, up to overnight, squishing them around every few hours to make sure the wings remain evenly coated.

3 Use a slotted spoon to transfer the wings to a colander in the sink. Let them drain for about 10 minutes.

4 Meanwhile, add 3 inches (7.5 cm) oil to a large, deep pot, set it over high heat, and bring it to 350°F (180°C). Use a fry thermometer for this.

5 Combine the rice flour, all-purpose flour, cornstarch, and baking powder in a large bowl.

6 Working in batches, add the wings to the bowl and toss them in the flour mixture until fully coated. Shake off the excess flour and drop the wings in the hot oil, making sure they are completely submerged. Fry until they are a deep, golden brown and fully cooked through, about 7 minutes, adjusting the heat as necessary to maintain 350°F (180°C). Transfer the fried wings to a paper towel–lined tray, and repeat with the remaining wings, adding more oil to the pot if needed.

7 Meanwhile, add the unused fish sauce marinade and the sriracha (if using) to a small pot over medium-high heat, and bring it to a boil. Reduce the heat to medium-low and simmer until the mixture become thick and syrupy and reduces to ⅔ cup (160 ml), 5 to 10 minutes. Remove from the heat.

8 Add the fried wings to a large bowl. Pour the reduced fish sauce mixture over the wings, and toss to combine. Top with Frizzled Shallots and scallions, and serve with lime wedges on the side.

SPECIAL EQUIPMENT
Fry thermometer

PREP AHEAD
Marinate the wings 1 day in advance. Store in the fridge.

PORK RIBS
with Swayze Sauce
serves 8 to 10

Nothing goes with Swayze Sauce better than these ribs. Not even Jennifer Grey. Don't forget to remove the membranes from the ribs; it's an important step. To do so, flip over each rack so the bones are facing up, slide your finger or a small knife underneath the edge of the membrane, and pull up and out to peel it off. Sometimes ribs come pre-peeled; confirm this with your butcher so you don't waste time trying to peel a membrane that isn't there. You can also ask the butcher to peel the membrane for you, but it's quite satisfying to do on your own. We nestle these ribs in a foil cradle for a few reasons: to keep the edges from burning, to hold them in the rendered fat like a bath so they get extra succulent, and to allow the uncovered tops to darken and caramelize. Easily scale this recipe up or down by adding or taking away racks. Depending on their size, two racks usually feed two to three people. If you like, finish the ribs on the grill instead of the oven in step 5. Baste and flip them a few times over high heat until they are charred, 5 to 7 minutes. When you serve them, be sure to put them in the middle of the table, because nobody puts baby back ribs in the corner.

4 racks pork baby back ribs (about 2 to 2½ pounds/907 to 1.1 kg each), back membranes removed

Kosher salt and freshly ground black pepper

Swayze Sauce (page 42)

1 Preheat the oven to 300°F (150°C). Line two large, rimmed baking sheets with a double layer of foil. Lay out four double layers of foil on your work surface, each layer big enough to (you guessed it!) hold a single rack of ribs. They don't need to completely cover the tops of the ribs; they just need to fold up along the sides, like a cradle.

2 Season the ribs liberally with salt and pepper, and place them bone side down on each of the foil sheets. Fold the foil up snugly along the edges of the ribs.

3 Transfer the ribs to the baking sheets. You should be able to fit two racks per sheet; if not, add more baking sheets as needed.

4 Bake the ribs for about 3 hours, until you can easily slide a paring knife through the meat between the bones. You want them to retain a little bit of structure, but not too much.

5 Remove from the oven, and bump up the heat as high as it will go—between 500°F and 550°F (260°C and 288°C). Press the foil down, if needed, so the full rib rack is exposed. Brush the tops liberally with Swayze Sauce, and blast in the oven for 5 to 7 minutes, until the tops are charred in spots.

6 Remove from the oven, let the ribs cool for a few minutes, and then slice and serve with extra Swayze Sauce on the side.

PREP AHEAD
Prep the ribs through step 4 up to 2 days in advance. Store, tightly wrapped, in the fridge. Bake from chilled, uncovered, according to step 5. You may need to add on a few extra minutes of cook time.

HACKABLE
Use store-bought barbecue sauce instead of the Swayze Sauce.

CUCUMBER SALAD BOATS

serves 8

This light and messy side dish balances the meaty richness of the sticky wings and ribs. Top these with sliced pepperoncini, sport peppers, or pickled jalapeños for added spice.

8 Persian cucumbers

Kosher salt

6 radishes, finely diced

3 Roma tomatoes or 1 large heirloom tomato, seeded and finely diced

2 to 3 tablespoons chopped fresh parsley, chives, dill, marjoram, or oregano (or any combination of herbs you like)

1 teaspoon fresh lemon juice

Freshly ground black pepper

Olive oil

1 cup (240 g) labneh or Greek yogurt

Large, flaky salt

1 Slice the cucumbers in half lengthwise, and scoop out the seeds. Season the insides with kosher salt, and set aside for 10 minutes to allow the salt to draw out some moisture.

2 Combine the radishes, tomatoes, herbs, and lemon juice in a small bowl. Season with salt and pepper, and drizzle with a touch of olive oil.

3 Use a paper towel to pat the cucumbers dry, inside and out. Fill each cucumber with the labneh, and top it with the radish-and-tomato mixture, straining off any liquid the vegetables may have produced. Sprinkle with the flaky salt and a few grinds of pepper, and serve immediately.

SPUMONI ICE CREAM CAKE

serves 10 to 12

Spumoni is a molded Italian dessert made with pistachio, cherry, and either chocolate or vanilla gelato. The colors are beautiful, and the flavor is buonissimo. In fact, the spumoni color palette was an early callout for this book's design. TBD if that panned out; as of this writing, we haven't started the design process. *Update: We are now in the copy editing phase and still haven't agreed on the color palette for the book. It's causing quite a bit of stress among the executives!* This cake may seem difficult to pull off, but it's actually easy because all the components are store-bought. All you have to do is assemble. The ice cream can take anywhere from 5 to 20 minutes to soften, depending on quality and room temperature. To speed it along and make sure it softens evenly, add the ice cream to a large bowl and use a thick metal spatula or spoon to chop it up and stir it around, à la Cold Stone Creamery. It should be the consistency of a thick porridge. If the cake or the ice cream pints ever get too melty, toss them in the freezer until they are firm enough to work with, usually around 30 minutes. This is a great basic recipe for any ice cream cake; experiment with other flavors, if you like. (Ahem…Neapolitan.) *This brings us to our final design update: We landed on mint chip with a hint of Neapolitan.* Some would argue that these colorways are the same as spumoni. We argue that the tonal nuances of "pistachio" vs. "mint" and "cherry" vs. "strawberry" are quite distinct, and choosing the wrong color would result in a disaster of unprecedented scale, as far as book designs go. Anyway, our designer, Becky, definitely needs a vacation, but the executives are pleased. Hope you are, too!

3 pints (or one 1½-quart/1.4 kg carton) pistachio ice cream

Pan spray, for greasing

8 ounces (227 g) crisp chocolate, vanilla, or shortbread cookies

12 classic rectangular ice cream sandwiches, ½- to ¾-inch thick (13 to 19 mm)

3 pints (or one 1½-quart/1.4 kg carton) cherry ice cream

1 cup (125 g) maraschino cherries, drained and stemmed (from a 10-ounce/283 g jar)

1 Soften the pistachio ice cream to a spreadable consistency.

2 In the meantime, spray a 9 × 13-inch (23 × 33 cm) pan with pan spray and line it with a double layer of plastic wrap, being sure to leave at least 2 inches (5 cm) of overhang on all sides. (The pan spray helps the plastic to stick to the sides.)

3 Add the cookies to a plastic zipper-top bag, and use a rolling pin or mallet to crush them into crumbs. Layer the crushed cookies evenly in the bottom of the pan. Scoop the pistachio ice cream on top and use a spoon or offset spatula to spread it in an even layer. Press down firmly on the ice cream to make sure it adheres to the cookies. Place the pan in the freezer for about 30 minutes.

4 Meanwhile, prepare the ice cream sandwiches: Unwrap all the ice cream sandwiches, and place them on top of the pistachio ice cream. You'll need to cut a couple so they fill the entire pan. Place the pan back in the freezer for about 30 minutes while the cherry ice cream softens.

5 Soften the cherry ice cream, and spread 2 pints (or two-thirds of the carton) over the ice cream sandwiches. Add the cherries, and press down using the ice cream as glue. Top with the remaining cherry ice cream, and spread it into an even layer, letting the cherries peek out a little bit on top.

6 Cover the cake with plastic wrap, and freeze for at least 4 hours and up to 1 month.

7 Use the plastic wrap overhang to lift the cake out of the pan. Slice and serve. If the cake is hard to cut, let it sit for a few minutes, and warm the knife by running it under hot water and wiping it dry between slices.

FREEZABLE
(obvs)

SPECIAL EQUIPMENT
Rolling pin or mallet

PREP AHEAD
Make the cake up to 1 month in advance. Store in the freezer. Wrap well to prevent freezer burn and odors from creeping in.

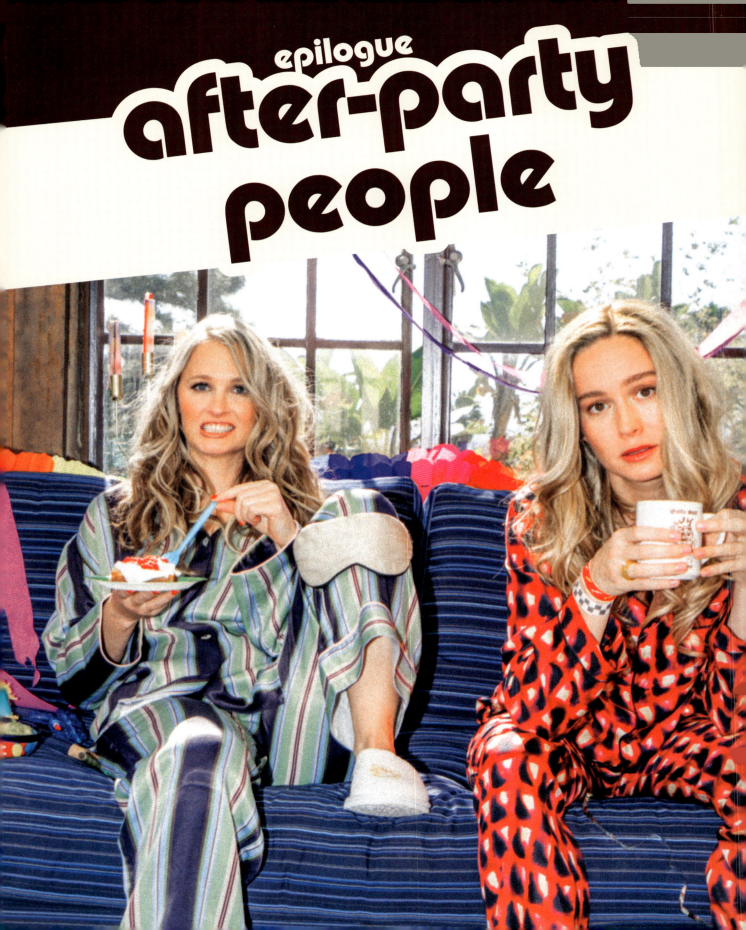

epilogue
after-party people

The sun has set on your party. Or maybe it's beginning to rise. Either way, it's over and you gotta face the consequences. Beyond doing the dishes, you'll probably need to deal with one heck of a hangover. According to science (we googled it), the entire body has to work overtime to process alcohol, and that's why you might wake up feeling like you caught a gnarly case of the brown bottle flu. The most effective way to avoid a hangover is to not drink, but although not all Party People imbibe, lots of them do, and we aren't here to tell you how to live your life. If you are among the affected, you will always run the risk of having one too many. Don't worry, you aren't alone; we've been there ourselves. Hangovers tend to affect people differently. For Courtney, it's the creeping anxiety; for Brie, it's the nausea. Other culprits include dehydration, headache, shakiness, moodiness, inflammation, sleep disruption, and depression. There are as many snake oil remedies for these symptoms as there are ways to get a hangover, but the only thing you can really do is ride it out and make yourself as comfortable as possible while you do. Above all, try not to be too hard on yourself. We all make mistakes, and sometimes having one or three too many is the mistake de la nuit. To be clear, we are not advocating drinking to the point that it irrecoverably harms you or the people you care about, nor are we touting alcoholism. Plus, there are tons of ways to have fun without booze. It's just that, like we said in the introduction, a good party creates a liminal space where everyone can feel safe to let loose, get silly, and make mistakes. Nowadays, it seems like the worst part of a hangover is the shame spiral it sends us into. We've stopped giving ourselves the grace to make questionable decisions, but questionable decisions are a part of life. Just because you have a hangover, it doesn't automatically mean you were bad. It probably just means you had a little too much fun. Take it easy the next day, and throw yourself an after-party. Slip into something cozy, grab a coloring book, and queue up your favorite TV show. Invite a couple friends over for a postmortem on last night's events, and make the After-Party People Detox Recovery Elixir (page 262) for your body to process along with all that booze. It will be over soon, and then you can start planning your next party. The worst hangover is the one you never had, so get out there and make us proud.

AFTER-PARTY PEOPLE DETOX RECOVERY ELIXIR

serves 2

No reason to beat around the bush: Once blended, this smoothie is a weird, skin-toned, pinkish, beige color. Add a few drops of red food coloring if you feel a certain kind of way about it. What it lacks in aesthetics, it more than makes up for in nutritional value, which is great because we didn't come here to look good; we came here to fight a hangover. All the ingredients are anti-inflammatory, high in antioxidants, and full of all sorts of vitamins and minerals. On top of this, turmeric fights muscle soreness and free radicals; chia seeds lower blood pressure; coconut water hydrates with electrolytes; cinnamon lowers blood sugar, improves cognitive function, and acts as an antimicrobial and antifungal agent; ginger and pineapple reduce nausea and indigestion; and kale activates detoxifying enzymes in the liver. So there.

2 cups (283 g) frozen pineapple chunks

2 cups (283 g) frozen strawberries

1 cup (28 g) baby kale

2 tablespoons peanut or almond butter

2 teaspoons chia seeds

½ teaspoon finely grated ginger

Large pinch ground cinnamon

Large pinch ground turmeric

2 cups (480 ml) coconut water

FOR SERVING

Four 200-mg ibuprofens

2 face masks

2 large iced coffees with CBD drops (for anxiety)

Probably some Breakfast Taco Casserole (page 245)

1 Add the pineapple, strawberries, kale, peanut butter, chia seeds, ginger, cinnamon, and turmeric to a blender. Cover with the coconut water, and blend until smooth.

2 Serve with the ibuprofen, face masks, and coffees. Make the Breakfast Taco Casserole when you've gathered enough strength. (Or just order a pizza.)

> **SPECIAL EQUIPMENT**
> Blender

index

Photo credits: pages 8, 28, 46, 51, 66, 70, 95, 96, 99, 101, 119, 140-141, 142, 143, 167, 182-183, 186, 190, 212, 213, 214, 218, 222-223, 234, 236, 246, 248-249, 260, 263, 272, endpapers © 2025 by Noah Fecks

pages 2, 20 © 2025 by Noah Paul

pages 10, 11, 12, 13 courtesy of the authors

All other images © 2025 by Ciarra Siller

acknowledgments

Endless thanks to:

Olivia Peluso, our editor: This book would not exist without you. Thank you for so clearly seeing our vision. From day one, you have given us the undying support to do our thing—which just so happens to also be your thing. :) From tracking down werewolf texture to attending our murder mystery party, you are an absolute treasure, a pure delight, and the truest Party Person there ever was. You also gifted us with LAsagna Garfield hats. Get used to these mugs; we aren't going anywhere!

The rest of the team at DK: our designer, Becky Batchelor; associate editor Brandon Buechley; art director Bill Thomas; copyeditor Christy Wagner; our extremely patient proofreaders, West Matuszak and Mira Park (sorry for any typos!); our indexer, Beverlee Day; and of course, CEO Paul Kelly, publisher Mike Sanders, VP of marketing Gayley Avery, publicity director Jennifer Brunn, and VP of sales Carol Stokke. Thank you from the bottom of our hearts. We love working with you and are beyond grateful.

Eve Attermann, our amazing agent, thank you for believing in us. Our big idea wasn't necessarily the easiest sell, but you made it look easy. And to the rest of our pals at WME—Rikki Bergman, Erin Malone, Chris Fioto, Meyash Prabhu, Madeline Whitesell, and Erin Junkin— we're looking at you!

Bee Berrie, you have our hearts forever. Thank you beyond. As the official Party People recipe tester and food stylist, you took our dreams and quite literally brought them to life. You are an ace, to put it mildly. To put it less mildly, we are obsessed with you.

Our fabulous kitchen brigade: Ben Baron, Alex Kofman, Daniel Choe, Matteo Connolly, and Courtney Weise. Your expertise, hard work, and knowledge of various cheese products raised this book to the next level.

Our photographer, Ciarra Siller, and our prop stylist, Hannah Lewis. Wow. Just wow. You nailed every shot and captured our vision in ways we didn't even think were possible. We can't thank you enough. What a special, magical team. We are literally tearing up as we write this.

Lizzie Pachter, Katie Rybacki, and Amy Rybacki, our dream team photo and prop assistants. You made every day on set a blast. Your creativity, calmness under pressure, and ability to find long-lost puzzle pieces are tops.

Noah Fecks, Ethan Lunkenheimer, Diego Gómez, Robert Byron Jones II, and Shannon Berkeley, our NYC-based lifestyle photographer and props team. We wish we didn't live so far apart. Thank you for coming all the way across the country to make beauty happen in LA. Long live the Andy Warhol Big Shot portraits!!

Our illustrious illustrator and bestie, Faye Orlove. Thank you for bringing the Party People archetypes to life. Jingle bell mazel tov!

Our Hot Dog Festival cohosts, Heather Edwards and Greg Gambina (who also happen to be Brie's parents). We love you so much. Heather, thank you for all of your support, including but not limited to sourcing props, building a stage, and coming through with various party rentals, decorations, general fun-time brilliance, and slushie-tasting expertise. You are the mother of parties, and we learned from the best.

Rebecca Orsak or, as we like to call you, the wind beneath our wings. Whether it's turning off house alarms at 3 a.m. or making a fake poison cocktail for a murder mystery, you are a Party Person through and through.

Dee and Randy Paul, you are angels sent from heaven above. Thank you for letting us raid your home for two full days. We promise to keep your fridge stocked with tasty treats forever.

Noah Paul, your BTS photos are front of scene in our hearts. Your talent is unparalleled. So is your hand modeling.

Speaking of hand models, many thanks to ours: Elise Shivamber, Allison Faulkner, Randall Stewart, Ben Baron, Noah Paul, Bee Berrie, Katie Rybacki, and Amy Rybacki.

Lee Eisenberg, thanks for lending us your incredible home. We owe you big time!

Orpha Ramirez, thanks for being our official recipe taster. <3

Samantha McMillen, Harley Vera Newton, Gelato Pique, Dorsey, The A-list, Samantha Pleet, Sleeper, L'Agence, Madewell, and J.Crew, for making us look stylish and chic.

Bryce Scarlett, Nina Park, Yukari Bush, Olga Pirmatova, Christopher Farmer, Jet Presley, Danni Katz, and Lili Kaytmaz for making our hair and faces look like we woke up like this. And by "like this," we mean stylish and chic.

Troy Bailey, Kyle Kuhns, Lindsay Galin, Maggie Bryant, Wallace Douglas, and Matt Pilipovich for helping this book soar far and wide.

Six-Thirty, Raffle, Toad, Obie, and Hamish—the best (and cutest) dogs we know. And also our cat friends, Henri, Nessa, Rue, Archie, and Rose Marie, who always hold it down for the feline party animal demographic.

Our nearest and dearest Party People, many of whose faces grace this book: Charlie Hodges, Megan Spell, Whitney Schmanski, Erin Sylvester, Liz Rubin, Bonnie Hunt Merrill, Johnny Merrill, Ant Hines, Laura Mulleavy, Kate Mulleavy, Nicolas Henderson, Daniel Choe, Mo Caulfield, Danny Baron, Jacqueline Novak, Chris Laker, Faye Orlove, Ross Cabbell, Jennifer Shapiro, Natalie Griffen, Rat, John Beck, Natalie Robehmed, Patrick Walker, Maria Larios, Taso Warsa, Gabriella Cetrulo, Noël Wells, Johnny Langan, Marlene Bailey, Eva Bailey, Wallace Douglas, Priya Manda, Christopher Farmer, Jet Presley, and 901.

Brie would personally like to thank Bonnie and Johnny Merrill for teaching her the beauty of family gatherings, chorizo, and Cards Against Humanity; her sister for being her inspiration in more ways than one; and Benjamin Styer for being the most passionate fruit carver, the MVP bartender, and the one she wants to party with until the end of time.

Court would personally like to thank her grandma (Grandmooh) for giving her *The Care Bears' Party Cookbook*; all of her parents for "liking" the black pepper hot dogs, Lawry's mashed potatoes, and any other weird concoctions she came up with as a child; and her sisters for putting up with her ridiculous shenanigans for literally decades. Plus a very special thanks to Ben White and Robot: One espresso martini is all it took. (Okay, well, maybe four.) She loves you both to the max.

And last but most definitely not least, we both give ultimate thanks to Martha Stewart and Garfield for raising us into the Party People we are today.

Psssst, hey, Brie, it's me, Courtney. Thanks for making this book with me! I couldn't ask for a better collaborator, friend, and Party Person sidekick than you. CHAIRS!!!

Courtney, it's Brie. I'm teary in the car reading your note. I love you endlessly, and I'm so proud of us, and I'm SO EXCITED to do a promo tour with you!

about the authors

Courtney McBroom is a Party Animal and Know-It-All hybrid. She's also a chef, a culinary producer, and the author of the cookbooks *Idiot Sandwich*, *Divine Your Dinner*, *All About Cake*, *Momofuku Milk Bar*, and *Milk Bar Life*. She is the founder of *Ruined Table*, a publishing and event series about dinner parties, and was the head food consultant for *Lessons in Chemistry* on Apple TV+. She is the former culinary director of Momofuku Milk Bar and has been a guest on shows such as *Chef's Table*, *The Mind of a Chef*, *Vice Munchies*, and *Bong Appétit*, and her writing and recipes have been featured in *Food & Wine*, *Vice*, *GQ*, *InStyle*, *Thrillist*, *Stylist*, and *Lucky Peach* magazine.

Descending from a long line of elaborate theme party enthusiasts, **Brie Larson** (a Host with the Most, with a Nostalgic One rising sign) can usually be found at Disneyland, her personal "Happiest Place on Earth." She is also known for winning an Academy Award for her lead performance in *Room*. Larson most recently costarred as "Margarita Rocks" in an at-home murder mystery party production, opposite family and friends. Professionally speaking, she also starred on stage in the West End production of *Elektra* and executive produced and led the Apple TV+ series *Lessons in Chemistry*, which earned her Emmy, SAG, Critics' Choice, and Golden Globe Award nominations. She is best known for her role as Carol Danvers/Captain Marvel in the Marvel superhero film franchise. Other big screen credits include *Fast X*, *The Glass Castle*, *Kong: Skull Island*, *Short Term 12*, *Trainwreck*, *The Spectacular Now*, *Don Jon*, and *Scott Pilgrim vs. the World*. She is also known for *United States of Tara*. She was named one of *TIME*'s 100 most influential people.